The Nuremberg Laws

Institutionalized Anti-Semitism

Titles in the
Words That Changed History series include:

Words
THAT
**CHANGED
HISTORY**

The
Nuremberg
Laws
Institutionalized
Anti-Semitism

by Amy Newman

Lucent Books
P. O. Box 289011, San Diego, CA 92198-9011

To Melvin, Deena, and Molly Libman,
for the miracle of friendship

Library of Congress Cataloging-in-Publication Data

Newman, Amy, 1970–
    The Nuremberg laws / by Amy Newman.
        p.   cm. — (Words that changed history)
    Includes bibliographical references and index.
    Summary: Chronicles the passage of the Nuremberg laws by the German
government in 1935 which denied basic human rights to millions of Jews,
Gypsies, and other minority groups.
    ISBN 1-56006-354-8 (lib. : alk. paper)
    1. Minorities—Legal status, laws, etc.—Germany—History—Juvenile
literature.   2. Race discrimination—Law and legislation—Germany—
History—Juvenile literature.   3. Jews—Legal status, laws, etc.—Germany—
History—Juvenile literature.   4. National socialism—Juvenile literature.
5. Minorities—Legal status, laws, etc.—Germany—History.   [1. Minorities—
Legal status, laws, etc.—Germany—History—Juvenile literature.   2. Race
discrimination—Law and legislation—Germany—History.   3. Jews—Legal
status, laws, etc.—Germany—History.   4. National socialism.]   I. Title.
II. Series: Words that changed history series.
KK4747.M55N49   1999
342.43'0873'09043—dc21   98-27778
                                                                                           CIP
                                                                                            AC

Copyright 1999 by Lucent Books, Inc.
P.O. Box 289011, San Diego, California 92198-9011

Printed in the U.S.A.

Contents

Foreword

"We hold these truths to be self-evident, that all men are created equal, that they are endowed by their Creator with certain unalienable Rights, that among these are Life, Liberty and the pursuit of Happiness." So states one of America's most cherished documents, the Declaration of Independence. These words ripple through time. They represent the thoughts of the Declaration's author, Thomas Jefferson, but at the same time they reflect the attitudes of a nation in which individual rights were trampled by a foreign government. To many of Jefferson's contemporaries, these words characterized a revolutionary philosophy of liberty. Many Americans today still believe the ideas expressed in the Declaration were uniquely American. And while it is true that this document was a product of American ideals and values, its ideas did not spring from an intellectual vacuum. The Enlightenment which had pervaded France and England for years had proffered ideas of individual rights, and Enlightenment scholars drew their notions from historical antecedents tracing back to ancient Greece.

In essence, the Declaration was part of an ongoing historical dialogue concerning the conflict between individual rights and government powers. There is no doubt, however, that it made a palpable impact on its times. For colonists, the Declaration listed their grievances and set out the ideas for which they would stand and fight. These words changed history for Americans. But the Declaration also changed history for other nations; in France, revolutionaries would emulate concepts of self-rule to bring down their own monarchy and draft their own philosophies in a document known as the Declaration of the Rights of Man and of the Citizen. And the historical dialogue continues today in many third world nations.

Lucent Books's Words That Changed History series looks at oral and written documents in light of their historical context and their lasting impact. Some documents, such as the Declaration, spurred people to immediately change society; other documents fostered lasting intellectual debate. For example, Charles Darwin's treatise *On the Origin of Species* did not simply extend the discussion of human origins, it offered a theory of evolution which eventually would cause a schism between some religious and scientific thinkers. The debate still rages as people on both sides reaffirm their intellectual positions, even as new scientific evidence continues to impact the issue.

Students researching famous documents, the time periods in which they were prominent, or the issues they raise will find the books in this series both compelling and useful. Readers will see the chain of events that give rise to historical events. They will understand through the examination of specific documents that ideas or philosophies always have their antecedents, and they will learn how these documents carried on the legacy of influence by affecting people in other places or other times. The format for the series emphasizes these points by devoting chapters to the political or intellectual climate of the times, the values and prejudices of the drafters or speakers, the contents of the document and its impact on its contemporaries, and the manner in which perceptions of the document have changed through time.

In addition to their format, the books in Lucent's Words That Changed History series contain features that enhance understanding. Many primary and secondary source quotes give readers insight into the thoughts of the document's contemporaries as well as those who interpret the document's significance in hindsight. Sidebars interspersed throughout the text offer greater examination of relevant personages or significant events to provide readers with a broader historical context. Footnotes allow readers to verify the credibility of source material. Two bibliographies give students the opportunity to expand their research. And an appendix that includes excerpts as well as full text of original documents gives students access to the larger historical picture into which these documents fit.

History is often shaped by words. Oral and written documents concretize the thoughts of a select few, but they often transform the beliefs of an entire era or nation. As Confucius asserted, "Without knowing the force of words, it is impossible to know men." And understanding the power of words reveals a new way of understanding history.

A Misuse of Law

Throughout history, laws have been used to prevent the strongest members of society from dominating the weakest. Without laws, the English philosopher John Locke observed, society returns to a "state of nature." In such a state, individuals who are strong enjoy many rights, and those who are weak enjoy very few.

Under the Nazis, Jews were forced to wear the Star of David to mark their status as pariahs and victims in a society defined by the Nuremberg Laws.

To ensure the rights of everyone—weak and strong alike—people band together to form a society. They replace the rule of might with the rule of law. Those who try to dominate others through brute strength—by stealing from them, for example, or raping them, or even killing them—are punished for these actions under the law. At certain times and in certain places, however, laws are used not to ensure the rights of all, but rather to allow some members of society to dominate others. Such is the case of the Nuremberg Laws of 1935.

Drafted by members of the Nazi Party in Germany, the Nuremberg Laws were designed to deny the most basic human rights to millions of Jews, Gypsies, and other minority groups. At the crux of the Nuremberg Laws was the notion that it is possible to categorize every person to one specific group. Thus, one was either a Jew or not a Jew, an Aryan or a non-Aryan. The Nuremberg Laws were not drafted to define the rights of people. Instead, they were designed to put prejudice into action. As such, these laws demonstrate the ways in which the legal system, in the hands of the wrong people, can be perverted and used to incite violence. The Nuremberg Laws stand as a monument to a time in which hatred was seen as the greatest good of a society. They remind posterity of the inevitable outcome of such a belief.

Sadly, the concepts embodied in the Nuremberg Laws—that people should be recognized by their differences rather than their similarities—did not disappear with the defeat of Nazi Germany in 1945.

CHAPTER 1 Denial and Adaptation

Even when he became the chancellor of Germany on January 30, 1933, Adolf Hitler was a hard man for many Germans to take seriously. He did not look at all like the racially pure Aryan *Übermenschen,* or supermen, whom he claimed would lead Germany into a new era of progress and power. His small stature, rounded shoulders, and toothbrush-like mustache gave him an almost comic appearance; Charlie Chaplin imitated him to great humorous effect in his film *The Great Dictator.* German citizen Friedrick Percyval Reck-Malleczewen, who wrote a book chronicling his experiences in the Nazi era, remarked that on seeing Adolf Hitler late one night in 1932 without a bodyguard, he easily could have shot and killed him:

> If I had had an inkling of the role this piece of filth was to play, and of the years of suffering he was about to make us endure, I would have done it without a second thought. But I took him for a character out of a comic strip, and did not shoot.[1]

Hitler's appearance was not the only thing about the man that struck many Germans as odd. His manner of public speaking also was unusual. His speeches were not the reasoned discussions of public policy that one expected from a national leader. They were more like emotional outbursts—bombastic, frenzied, filled with exaggeration and lies.

Hitler's ideas were as extreme as his speechmaking. For example, he blamed Germany's defeat in World War I on an international banking conspiracy led by Jews. According to Hitler, Jewish bankers lent money to the warring nations in a way that prevented any side from becoming strong enough to win. This lending practice, Hitler said, prolonged the war so the bankers could increase their profits. Hitler maintained that the Jewish bankers eventually tightened Germany's credit to the point that it could no longer afford to fight, causing the nation to lose the war.

Hitler was not the only German to hold these baseless beliefs, but he drew conclusions more extreme than those of most of his contemporaries. In his autobiographical polemic *Mein Kampf,* which he wrote in prison while serving time for attempting to overthrow the government in 1923, Hitler maintained that Jews should pay with their lives for their supposed betrayal of Germany:

Adolf Hitler's political party, which was filled with criminals, hoodlums, and drug addicts and which often met in beer halls, was looked on as a joke by the major political parties.

If at the beginning of the war, and during the war, 12,000 or 15,000 of these Hebrew defilers had been put under poison gas as hundreds of thousands of our very best workers from all walks of life had to endure at the front, then the sacrifice of millions would not have been in vain.[2]

Hitler's menacing words might have proved more worrisome to Jews in Germany had he been backed by a political party filled with respected politicians. He was not. The party he led, the *Nationalsozialistische Deutsche Arbeiterpartei* (NSDAP), known as the Nazi party, was filled with criminals, hoodlums, and drug addicts—society's outcasts. Horst Wessel, praised as the valiant party fighter who lent his name to the organization's most popular song, was killed by another man in an argument over a prostitute. The Nazis hardly seemed a threat to anyone but themselves.

A False Sense of Security

Because of Hitler's simpleminded ideas and outlandish rhetoric, many German Jews felt they could safely ignore him. After all, Germany was a civilized nation, a place where, for the most part, the rule of law, not mass hysteria and mob violence, prevailed. Although Hitler targeted the Jews for punishment in his speeches, few believed he would—or legally could—go any farther than that.

The sense of security felt by the Jews in Germany arose from the fact that when Hitler came to power they formed a firmly entrenched minority. Few German Jews experienced the sense of inferiority often felt by small groups in a large culture. According to Yehuda Bauer, Jews had lived in Germany for more than sixteen hundred years, long before the German nation even existed. More importantly, unlike Jews in other countries, the Jews of Germany had arrived, both economically and socially. For example, 15 percent of all German doctors were Jewish, a percentage thirty times higher than their representation in the population. An amazing 26 percent of all lawyers were Jewish. In the years prior to World War II, Jews accounted for eleven of the thirty-eight Nobel Prizes awarded to citizens of Germany, twenty-nine times their proportion in society.

German Jews like Paul Ehrlich, who developed a treatment for syphilis, brought recognition and honor to their country. When the Nazis came to power, his name would be erased from street signs.

German Jewish luminaries in many fields added prestige to their fatherland. Herman Mikowski, for example, advanced the idea of a four-dimensional time continuum. Tullio Levi-Civita developed absolute calculus, the mathematical instrument that Albert Einstein later used to develop his theories of relativity. German Jews helped improve the world's health with their inventions and discoveries. Waldemar Haffkine developed an inoculation against cholera. The test and treatment for syphilis were both discovered by Jews, August von Wasserman and Paul Ehrlich. When the Nazis came to power, they were anxious to erase all traces of the contributions Jews had made in Germany. For example, Frankfurt's Paul Ehrlich Strasse (street) was quickly renamed for Nazi leader Heinrich Himmler.

Hitler routinely maintained that the Jews as a group were responsible for Germany's defeat in World War I, but the nation's history contradicted this notion. Some 100,000 Jews fought for Germany in World War I. More than 10,000 died for the fatherland. German military records show that 35,000 Jews received decorations for bravery in battle.

Because of their many contributions to their nation and culture, Germany's Jews felt themselves to be as German as their Protestant and Catholic neighbors. Because they were well assimilated into society, many Jews denied the importance of Hitler's excesses. They misjudged the man and his followers. Hitler and the Nazi Party would need less than three years to oust German Jews from the society they loved.

Danger Signs

Shortly after taking power, Hitler took decisive steps to ensure that his policies were not opposed or even debated. On February 28, 1933, within a month of his chancellorship, Hitler's government issued decrees suspending the freedoms of press, speech, assembly, and privacy for all Germans. Newspapers, radio stations, book publishers, and motion picture producers were required to promote the doctrines of the Nazi Party. Anyone who openly challenged Nazi authority, in speech or in print, risked jail.

With their opposition silenced, the Nazis began an organized and nationwide attack on the Jews. Members of the *Sturmabteilung* (SA), an elite faction of the Nazi Party identified by their brown-shirted uniforms, began to harass Jews. They forced Jews to wash the streets under armed guard and subjected them to other indignities. These actions were not legal, but no one was willing to stop Hitler's brown-shirted henchmen. Hermann Göring, the Nazi official in charge of enforcing laws, explained the government's position on crimes against Jews in a speech delivered on March 12, 1933:

> Certainly, I shall employ the police and quite ruthlessly, whenever the German people are hurt; but I refuse the notion that the police are protective troops for Jewish stores. No, the police protect whoever comes into Germany legitimately, but it does not exist for the purpose of protecting Jewish usurers.[3]

To the Nazi faithful, the message was clear: The police would not stop them from attacking Jewish businesses.

The anti-Jewish actions of Hitler's new government shocked members of the press around the world. A spate of negative reports about Hitler's regime appeared in newspapers across Europe and in the United States. This criticism aroused the German chancellor's anger. As usual, Hitler blamed the Jews for his troubles.

On March 26, 1933, Hitler summoned Joseph Goebbels, his chief propagandist, and directed him to organize a boycott of Jewish stores. The purpose of the boycott was to stop unfavorable reports about the new Nazi government in the foreign press. Goebbels, a diligent diarist, recorded his thoughts after meeting with Hitler that day:

> We shall only be able to combat the falsehoods abroad if we get at those who originated them or at those Jews living in Germany who have remained thus far unmolested. We must, therefore, proceed to a large-scale boycott of all Jewish businesses in Germany. Perhaps the foreign Jews will think better of the matter when their racial comrades begin to get it in the neck.[4]

The boycott was not the only step the Nazis took to halt the negative press reports. On the same day that Hitler met with Goebbels, Göring summoned Jewish leaders to his office. He demanded that

Joseph Goebbels, the Nazi's chief propagandist, organized the Nazi boycott of Jewish businesses. He was a master manipulator, twisting facts to meet the Party's needs.

the German Jews contact Jewish organizations in other countries and deny the reports of attacks on Jews. Göring made it clear that this was not a friendly request; failure to meet his demands would result in more violence against Jews.

The leaders of Jewish organizations decided to appease Göring. They immediately sent telegrams to their supporters overseas, telling them the reports about conditions in Germany were false. The president of Berlin's Jewish community pleaded for the cooperation of the American Jewish community:

> According to newspaper reports, atrocity and boycott propaganda against Germany is continuing overseas, apparently also in part by Jewish organizations. As Germans and Jews we must enter a decisive protest against this. The dissemination of untrue reports can only bring harm, affecting the reputation of our German fatherland, endangering the relations of the German Jews with their fellow citizens. Please try urgently to see to it that every atrocity and boycott propaganda report is halted.[5]

Goebbels also worked quickly. Two days after his meeting with Hitler, a group he had formed, the Central Committee for Defense Against Jewish Atrocity and Boycott Propaganda, announced a boycott of Jewish stores to be held on April 1. To make sure the German public supported the boycott, teams of *Schutzstaffel* (SS) (protective squads) and *Sturmabteilung* (SA) (storm detachment) guards were stationed in front of Jewish stores. The Nazi soldiers warned would-be patrons not to enter the stores.

Once the Nazi government made it clear that it would not defend the rights of Jews, anyone with a bias against Jews felt free to take action against them. For example, many Germans resented the fact that a disproportionately large number of Jews held positions of authority in the judicial system. Shortly after Göring's speech about not defending Jews, SA men in the city of Breslau broke into the local courthouse, seized Jewish judges and lawyers, and dragged them through the streets. Instead of defending the Jews who had been attacked, officials in the Department of Justice in Breslau announced that they would accede to "the wishes of the people" by forcing Jewish judges and lawyers from their jobs.

Breslau was not the only place where Jewish judges and lawyers came under attack. Several German states acted to limit Jewish involvement in the judiciary. In Bavaria, the Ministry of Justice ordered that Jewish judges not be allowed to rule on criminal and disciplinary cases. In Prussia, Minister of Justice Hans Kerrl issued a statement

To the Nazis, Jews were enemies who must be fought in any way possible. SA and SS guards blocked the entrances to Jewish-owned stores, which were also marked with signs like this one: "Germans! Defend yourselves! Do not buy from Jews!"

that called for all Jewish judges to retire by April 1, 1933. Kerrl announced that judges who did not comply with the request would be physically barred from entering the courthouse. Furthermore, Kerrl ordered that Jews no longer be permitted to serve on juries. He also decreed that the number of Jewish lawyers allowed to practice law be proportionate to their percentage in the German population. By March 1933, hundreds of Jews had been forced from their jobs by a combination of violence and administrative actions.

The attacks on Jewish lawyers meant that non-Jewish lawyers gained many new clients, since a large number of Jewish lawyers

Hindenberg Protest

When Paul von Hindenberg, the German president who appointed Adolf Hitler chancellor, learned of the dismissals of Jewish civil servants and jurists, he wrote a letter to the Nazi leader. Hindenberg maintained that the Nazi activities against Jewish veterans were a disgrace to the German army. Lucy S. Dawidowicz quotes the letter in her 1975 book, *The War Against the Jews 1933–1945:*

> In the last few days a whole series of cases have been reported to me in which war-wounded judges, lawyers, and civil servants in the judiciary, with unblemished records of service, have been forcibly furloughed and will later be dismissed simply because they are of Jewish origin. For me personally, revering those who died in the war and grateful to those who survived and to the wounded who suffered, such treatment of Jewish war veterans in the civil service is altogether intolerable. I am convinced that you, Herr Chancellor, share these human feelings and therefore I most sincerely urge you to concern yourself with this matter and to see to it that an honorable solution for the entire civil service is found. I believe that civil servants, judges, teachers, and lawyers who were wounded in the war or fought at the front, or are sons of those who died or had sons die in battle must—insofar as they have not given cause to be treated otherwise—be allowed to continue in their professions. If they were worthy to fight and bleed for Germany, then they should also be considered worthy to continue serving the fatherland in their professions.

Hindenberg was not speaking out of concern for the Jews. He had no qualms about dismissing Jews who had not served in the war. What mattered to him was the morale of the German military and the general spirit of patriotism. Hindenberg worried that shabby treatment of war veterans would undermine the spirit of self-sacrifice so important to a nation preparing for all-out war.

Hindenberg did not mind if the Nazis oppressed the Jews, so long as they were not military veterans like him.

ould no longer practice their profession. The Jews lost more than business and income, however. More importantly, they lost their influence in the judicial system—the one area of the government that could protect their rights. Barred from juries and stripped of their ability to advocate their rights in court, German Jews were left to the mercy of the non-Jewish population.

Official Sanctions

Not content with the haphazard firings of judges and lawyers, on April 2 the German government passed the Law for the Restoration of the Professional Civil Service. This law authorized the removal of Jews and others who opposed the Nazis from civil service jobs, effectively blocking Jews from working in all areas of public life—schools, transportation, communications, government, and law.

The drive to remove Jews from public life was the first board in the fence the Nazis would build around the Jews, separating them from the Germany in which they felt they belonged so completely. The actions against the Jews met with little resistance on the part of depression-strapped Germans, many of whom were happy to have access to jobs that became available. The Jews, for their part, had already learned from the boycott and Göring's threats that protesting the Nazi actions was useless. They could not speak out in the press or in public, or even assemble to discuss what to do. Nor could they appeal to the courts for justice. Without recourse against the attacks, the Jews tried, as they had throughout their long history, to adapt to the adverse conditions.

Adaptation was not easy, as conditions continued to change rapidly. On April 7 the Nazis passed a decree stating that Jews were no longer allowed to work as lay assessors and jurors, extending a Prussian ban to the rest of the country. On April 22, Jews were barred from employment as physicians in social service institutions. On April 25 the Nazis passed the Law Against the Overcrowding of German Schools and Institutions of Higher Learning. This law effectively barred Jews from attending German schools. The Jews responded by organizing new schools for Jewish pupils, led by teachers who had lost their jobs under the Law for the Restoration of the Professional Civil Service. But each new adaptation was at best a reprieve until the Nazis moved to erect the next part of the fence isolating them from German society.

On May 6 the Law for the Restoration of the Professional Civil Service was further extended, taking away the livelihood of Jewish professors and notaries. On June 2 the Jews received notice that they could no longer be dentists or dental technicians, either.

Between 1933 and 1935, some 60,000 Jews, including this family, left Germany in response to the growing acts of oppression.

After six months of persecution, many Jews stopped denying what was happening to their society and began to emigrate to other countries. Between 1933 and 1935, approximately sixty thousand Jews left Germany. Most Jews, however, still tried to adapt to the changing political climate. Although the space in which Jews could move in German society was becoming increasingly smaller, the Jews tried to make a tolerable life for themselves.

In addition to the economic and social isolation that was being forced upon the Jews, June 1933 saw the birth of a new kind of isolation—the concentration camp. A detention facility known as

Dachau was opened near Munich, a place where the Nazis could detain political foes, religious dissenters, and Jews. In time, Dachau would be followed by similarly notorious camps at Buchenwald, Sachsenhausen, and Ravensbrück.

Heinrich Class

German anti-Semitism did not originate with Hitler and the Nazi Party. The Nazis followed in the footsteps of the anti-Semitic politicians who came before them. One such Jew hater was Heinrich Class. In 1912, he wrote a book called *If I Were King* (*Wenn Ich der Kaiser Wär*) that served as a checklist for Nazi lawmakers. In *The War Against the Jews 1933–1945*, Lucy Dawidowicz quotes a portion of the book in which Class described the decrees he would issue if he were king:

> All public offices, whether, national, state, or municipal, salaried or honorary, are closed to Jews. Jews are not admitted to serve in the army or navy. Jews have neither an active nor a passive right to vote. The occupation of lawyer and teacher is forbidden to them, also the direction of theaters. Newspapers on which Jews work must make that known; newspapers that may be called "German" are not permitted to be owned by Jews or to have Jewish managers or coworkers. Banks that are not purely personal enterprises are not permitted to have any Jewish directors.

> In the future rural property may not be owned by Jews or mortgaged by them. As compensation for the protection that Jews enjoy as aliens, they must pay double the taxes that Germans pay. . . .

> Today, the borders must be totally and unconditionally barred to any further Jewish immigration. This is absolutely necessary, but no longer sufficient. Just as self-evident, foreign Jews who have not yet acquired citizenship rights must be speedily and unconditionally expelled, to the last man. But this also is not enough. . . . We must demand that resident Jews be placed under an Aliens' Law. . . .

> A Jew, according to the above Aliens' Law, is anyone who belonged to a Jewish religious corporation as of 18 January 1871, as well as all the descendants of such persons who were Jews at that date, even when only one parent was or is [a Jew by the above definition].

Despite all the changes in German society in the first six months of the Nazi regime, some German Jews took comfort in the fact that despite the changes they remained German citizens. Though their rights as citizens had been diminished, they had not vanished. Many German Jews held out the hope that their rights as citizens might be restored in the future. For many, this hope vanished on July 14, 1933, the day the Nazis passed the Law on the Revocation of Naturalization and Annulment of German Citizenship. This law annulled, or canceled, the citizenship of people the Nazis termed "undesirables." This law was used to strip away the citizenship of the many Eastern European Jews who had immigrated to Germany after the end of World War I.

Throughout the fall of 1933, the fence around the Jews grew higher. Government authorities were no longer allowed to employ Jews or their spouses. Jews also were excluded from participating in any cultural or entertainment endeavors. The National Press Law put all political newspapers under the supervision of the government. This meant that the Law for the Restoration of the Professional Civil Service now applied to journalists. Jews who worked for newspapers and magazines lost their jobs. Jews also were barred from inheriting farmland. The pace of emigration continued as more and more Jews found it impossible to live in the new Germany.

Many Jewish organizations found themselves shut down or severely curtailed by the authorities. Jews could not belong to German sports clubs, art circles, or academic societies. The Nazis did allow one type of Jewish organization to operate unhampered, however: the Zionists.

Zionist groups were centered around the idea that the goal of all Jews should be to form a Jewish state in Palestine Most German Jews were not Zionists. Their primary loyalty was to Germany. Some demonstrated this belief in statements such as "Stuttgart is our Jerusalem."[6] With the coming of the Nazis, however, membership in Zionist groups grew. The Nazis did not discourage membership in these groups. Zionism united Jews and Nazis under a common goal: to get Jews out of Germany.

A Temporary Reprieve

The hopes of Jewish leaders who had preached tolerance and adaptation to the new realities were bolstered by the events of 1934. Only two major anti-Jewish laws were passed that year. On January 24, Jews were banned from membership in the German Labor Front, a major labor union. On May 17, Jews were no longer eligible for national health insurance. As the pace of persecution slowed,

German Jews took stock of their lives and attempted to make conditions as livable as possible. The respite was only temporary, however.

In 1935 anti-Jewish violence erupted again. There were more boycotts of Jewish businesses and more physical attacks on Jews. Jews were prevented from going to cinemas, visiting the theater, or finding recreation at public swimming pools and resorts. Again, news of the violence against the Jews led to an outcry in foreign countries. Many nations refused to do business with Germany, and this posed problems for the German economy. Hjalmar Schacht, the president of Germany's federal bank, the Reichsbank, was so concerned by the decline in trade that he decided to take action. On August 10, 1935, he spoke out against random violence against Jews:

> No one in Germany is without rights. . . . The Jew can become neither a citizen nor a fellow German. But . . . he must not be under arbitrary action, but under the law.[7]

Two days later, Schacht convened a meeting of the heads of the departments of the Ministry of Economy to discuss the effects of what he called "Jew-baiting" on the German financial situation. Minister of

Signs marked places of recreation, like this public swimming pool, where Jews were forbidden to enter after 1935.

Zionism

Within the Nuremberg Laws is found a small paragraph that denies Jews the right to fly the Nazi flag, but permits them to raise the Jewish colors (the Zionist flag). When the Nazis cracked down on all forms of Jewish social life, they left the Zionist groups unmolested. The Nazis fully supported the Zionist aim of resettling Jews in the area then known as Palestine, which is now Israel.

Before the Nazis came to power, few German Jews felt much Zionist fervor. Most assimilated Jews thought that Zionism made suspect their loyalty to their home country. German Jews, for the most part, agreed with the sentiments expressed by the French Jewish leader Abraham Furtado. In *The Course of Modern Jewish History,* Howard Morley Sachar quotes Furtado when Jews were emancipated in France:

> We no longer form a nation within a nation. France is our country. Jews, such today is your status. Your obligations are outlined, your happiness is waiting.

German-Jewish leaders insisted that they were not German Jews, but merely Germans of the Jewish faith. When the First World Zionist Congress met in 1897, the Jewish leaders in western Europe wholeheartedly opposed it. They did not agree with the Zionist goal of creating a political state, believing that such a stand contradicted the notion that Judaism was legitimately a religion, not a political construct.

Eastern Jews, who had no history of emancipation or assimilation, led the movement to form a Jewish homeland. When the Nuremberg Laws equalized the position of the assimilated German Jews with that of their Eastern coreligionists, German support for Zionism suddenly grew. Until the Nazis closed off Jewish emigration, the Zionists worked diligently to bring as many German Jews to Palestine as possible.

the Interior Wilhelm Frick, who was at the meeting, introduced an order he had drafted that contradicted Göring's policy of not protecting Jews against violence. Frick's order called for the police to get involved when "illegal actions" were taken against Jews. (Government-ordered actions were another matter entirely.) The heads of the departments discussed Frick's order, but they refused to endorse it. They worried that such action might be seen as an admission of how severe the violence against Jews had become. They also did not like the idea of bowing to pressure over the Jews.

Frick left the meeting still convinced that random violence against Jews was damaging the German government. His interest was not in protecting Jews, but in making sure that the government's reputation did not suffer. The image of a lawful society must be maintained if the new German government was to thrive. Whatever was going to be done to the Jews must be done legally. Wilhelm Frick would see to that himself. He knew that the laws that had been passed so far were only the beginning; more legislation was in the works that would further define the place of Jews in German society. Among them were Frick's most effective legislation: the Nuremberg Laws.

Putting Prejudice into Action

In the spring of 1937, some members of the Nazi Party felt that Adolf Hitler had not done enough to remove the Jews from German society. Hitler told his followers to be patient. He explained that the actions taken against the Jews up to that time, including the passage of the Nuremberg Laws, were all part of a grand strategy. "I do not summon an enemy with force to fight," he explained. "I don't say: 'Fight!' because I want to fight. Instead I say, 'I will destroy you!' And now, wisdom, help me to maneuver you into the corner that you cannot fight back, and then you get the blow to the heart."[8] The Nuremberg Laws allowed Hitler to maneuver the Jews into a corner from which they could not fight back.

For the millions of Jews in Germany and in the countries that fell under German control during World War II, the Nuremberg Laws meant the difference between an honorable career and unemployment, between comfort and penury, and ultimately between life and death. These powerful laws had humble beginnings.

Humble Beginnings

On September 13, 1935, Hitler decided to introduce major anti-Jewish legislation at a special session of the Reichstag, or German parliament, at the end of the annual NSDAP congress in Nuremberg. Nazi Party officials had succeeded in drafting only one law, however—a decree that would forbid Jews from displaying the Nazi flag, the swastika. This minor law did not make the spectacular statement Hitler had in mind for a party congress that would be filled with torchlight parades, rabble-rousing speeches at Zeppelin Field, goose-stepping Hitler Youth, and crowds of adoring Germans. Instead, Hitler ordered Wilhelm Frick, his minister of the interior, to prepare legislation that would regulate the relationship between Jews and non-Jews—the German-Jewish "blood relationship." From this order would come the Nuremberg Laws.

The Legal Mind

Hitler gathered a talented group of subordinates charged with turning his ideas into the force of a popular movement that would inspire an entire nation to action. He could hardly have chosen a better candidate

Minister of the Interior Wilhelm Frick allowed his legal and administrative talents to be misused by Hitler. He wrote effective laws that helped tear apart the German legal system and spelled the doom for most of European Jewry.

to spearhead the creation of the Nuremberg Laws than Wilhelm Frick. Historian Eugene Davidson writes of Frick, "The laws and decrees he would . . . draw up had staying power."[9]

With a doctorate in law and a strong middle-class background, Frick seemed an unlikely individual to become involved with the Nazi Party, which had the stated aim of overturning the rule of law in Germany and included many criminals among its members. Frick shared one important trait with the Nazis, however: he resented Jews. He believed the Jews had become too influential and powerful in German society. When Frick met Adolf Hitler, he found someone who not only shared the same beliefs but wanted to act on them. Frick became a true believer in the Nazi cause. An examination of the party's early history reveals that Frick was always in the thick of things. In fact, Frick is one of only nine men listed in an index titled "Old Comrades in Arms" that appears in *Mein Kampf.* He earned his place there.

When Hitler attempted an unsuccessful coup to take over the Bavarian government in November 1923, Frick was serving as an official in the Munich police department. He gave orders not to use police force against Hitler and the other members of the putsch. His loyalty to Hitler earned him one year and three months in Landsberg prison for treason and gross breach of duty.

This was not Frick's first illegal act of loyalty to the Nazi Party. In 1921 he had issued fake passports to Nazis fleeing murder charges.

Frick's familiarity with the German bureaucracy and his willingness to help the NSDAP had huge implications. Without Frick, Hitler would have been ineligible under German law to become chancellor. Hitler had renounced his Austrian citizenship in 1925, and Frick worked tirelessly to obtain German citizenship for his führer, or leader. Finally, in 1932, Frick succeeded in getting Hitler named as a councillor in Braunschweig, a position that included automatic German citizenship.

Frick came to Hitler's aid again one year later. In 1933, after Hitler had been named chancellor of Germany, a fire of mysterious origin swept through the Reichstag building. Hitler blamed the fire on members of the Communist Party, who he claimed were attempting to overthrow the government. To counteract the supposed threat from the Communists, Hitler demanded what amounted to dictatorial powers. Frick helped Hitler obtain the powers he sought.

Frick drafted the Law for Removing the Distress of People and Reich, also known as the Enabling Act. The Enabling Act, which Frick signed in his capacity as minister of the interior, gave Hitler the power to make laws without the approval of the Reichstag. In essence, Frick gave Hitler what historian Joseph Persico calls "the

Before the Nazis came to power, the paramilitary arm of the Party, the SA, staged raids on their opponents, like this one in Munich, November 9, 1923.

Wilhelm Frick

Wilhelm Frick was at the forefront of the Nazi Party. In fact, he was the first Nazi to hold political office when he attained a provincial post in Thuringia. Once ensconced, he used his political power to get other party members appointed to government jobs.

The first piece of legislation Frick introduced after his election in 1924 was a bill that would have excluded Jews from all public office. He also was an ardent supporter of party efforts to prevent people with hereditary diseases from bearing children. To that end, he drafted the law that required the sterilization of people with such conditions. In *The War Against the Jews 1933–1945,* Lucy S. Dawidowicz relates Frick's statement at the first meeting of the Council of Experts on Population and Race Policy in the summer of 1933:

> Only when the state and the public health authorities will strive to make the core of their responsibilities the provision for the yet unborn, then we can speak of a new era and of a reconstructed population and race policy.

Frick's star was at its apex when the Nuremberg Laws were passed. Thereafter, his importance waned because most of the administrative and legal tasks he was skilled at were accomplished. Throughout the rest of the Third Reich, Frick continued to lose power to other Nazis with a greater taste for violence. He did not, however, ever lose his place in the inner circle of the Nazi Party. For example, in the fall of 1939, Frick was named as one of only six members of the German war cabinet.

To the end, Frick remained loyal to Adolf Hitler and the party's ideals. On trial for his life at the International Military Tribunal in Nuremberg after the war, Frick refused to speak in his own defense.

He never recanted his support of the beliefs of the Nazis. Observers at the trial found it hard to believe that Frick had been a top Nazi. In *Infamy on Trial,* Joseph Persico writes, "Among the defendants in the dock, Wilhelm Frick was the invisible man, his only feature being the incongruous checkered jacket he wore every day."

In jail after the war, awaiting trial for war crimes and crimes against humanity, Frick still believed in the Nazi cause.

patina [appearance] of legality to despotism."[10] Frick saw nothing wrong with his service to Hitler and the Nazi Party. Years later, on trial for crimes against humanity, Frick commented, "I believe I have deserved punishment no more than have the tens of thousands of faithful German servants and officials in the public service who have already been detained in camps for over a year merely because they did their duty."[11]

The Bureaucrats

Two men who "did their duty" by helping Frick draft the Nuremberg Laws were Hans Pfundtner and Wilhelm Stuckart, functionaries at the Ministry of Interior. Little is known of Stuckart and Pfundtner. These men, like thousands of other faceless bureaucrats who made the Nazi state operate efficiently, went into action, writing version after version of the Nuremberg Laws from the morning of September 14, 1935, until 3:00 A.M. on September 15. Different versions of the laws were shuttled to Hitler, who commented on them and then sent the men back to work.

Apparently the work of Stuckart gained Hitler's approval. Years later, the German dictator called on Stuckart to write another law that would radically alter the status of a large group of people. In March 1938, Stuckart rushed to Vienna to draft a law making Austria a province of Germany. Stuckart also represented the Ministry of Interior at the Wannsee Conference of 1942, the meeting at which the so-called final solution, or extermination of the Jews, was planned and set in motion.

The Theorist

A final person completed the team that would write the laws disenfranchising Germany's Jews from sixteen hundred years of their history. His name was Bernard Lösener. An expert in "racial law," Lösener flew in from Berlin with ministry files to help draft the Nuremberg Laws. Lösener previously had served the German nation as a customs official. He had spent several years examining goods coming into the country, categorizing and grading them according to set rules. As he worked on the Nuremberg Laws, Lösener viewed human beings much as he had shipments of goods. In the course of his career, he wrote twenty-seven decrees categorizing people based on their race.

Not content with legalizing prejudice and hatred, the Nazis strove to put a gloss of scholarship and respectability on their racial theories. In fact, the Nazis went so far as to found the Academy of German Law, an institution designed to provide "data" to back up anti-Semitic decrees and legislation, including the Nuremberg Laws.

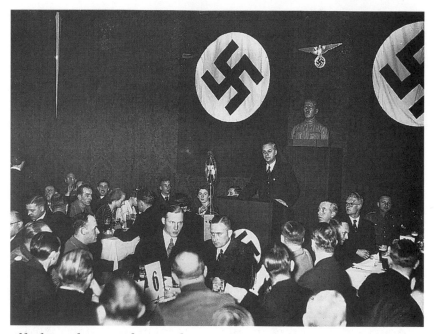

Alfred Rosenberg, seen here speaking at a Nazi Party dinner, was one of the chief "racial theorists" of the Nazi Party. He recruited academics to create a "Science of Racism."

According to Paul Johnson, the Nazis took over the college campuses years before they took over the country. Their ideas found willing listeners among college students, and faculty members turned their intellects toward creating a "scientific basis" for Nazi ideals. Adolf Hitler named his adviser Alfred Rosenberg Commissioner of the Führer for the Supervision of the Total Intellectual and Philosophical Schooling and Training of the National Socialist Party. His job was to recruit theorists, professors, and others in the academic professions to create what he termed a "Science of Racism."[12]

Rosenberg is most famous for elaborating the concept of *Lebensraum,* which stated that a nation needed a certain amount of space to be self-sufficient. *Lebensraum* would be used by the Nazis as a justification for the German invasion of neighbor states during the war.

A Unique Vision

Despite the fact that a committee worked to write the laws and the legislature voted to approve them, the Nuremberg Laws embodied Adolf Hitler's unique form of anti-Semitism and incorporated many of his idiosyncrasies. For example, among the Nuremberg Laws is a clause stating that no Aryan woman younger than age forty-five could be employed in a Jewish home. One need only look into Adolf's family history to learn the origin of this law. When she was forty-two and working as a cook in the home of a well-to-do Jewish family, Hitler's grandmother Anna Schicklgruber had become pregnant out of wedlock.

Rubber Stamp

On September 15, 1935, Adolf Hitler approved the efforts of Frick, Stuckart, Pfundtner, and Lösener. The disparate statutes that came to be known as the Nuremberg Laws went to the Reichstag for approval. On trial for his life a little over a decade later, Hermann Göring was asked, "To what extent did you participate in issuing the Nuremberg Laws of 1935?" He replied, "In my capacity as president of the Reichstag, I promulgated those Laws, here in Nuremberg, where the Reichstag was meeting at the time."[13] Göring flattered himself. His participation was unneeded. Hitler had the power under the Enabling Act to make laws without the Reichstag. He used the vote in the Reichstag merely to provide a more impressive debut for laws which in large part only codified practices already in effect. On September 15, 1935, the Reichstag voted to enact both the Reich Citizenship Law and the Law for the Protection of

As was the case with all Nazi Party activities, Adolf Hitler was firmly in control of the creation and passage of the Nuremberg Laws.

German Blood and German Honor. These two laws, along with a decree enacted November 14, 1935, that defined the status of *Mischlinge,* or people of mixed heritage, made up the Nuremberg Laws.

The Reich Citizenship Law

The Reich Citizenship Law defined a German citizen as anyone who "enjoys the protection of the German Reich and for this reason is specifically obligated to it." "The Reich citizenship is the sole bearer," the laws stated further, "of full political rights as provided by the laws."[14]

The Reich Citizenship Law consisted of two parts. The first part of the law referred to the race, or "blood," of a person; the second part of the law referred to the person's conduct: A Reich citizen is only that subject of German or kindred blood who proves by his conduct that he is willing and suited loyally to serve the German people and the Reich.[15]

This law stripped Jews and Gypsies of their citizenship, because they were not of German blood. It did not matter that these "foreign" people had lived on German soil for hundreds of years. With the swipe of a pen, they lost the rights and protections that come with citizenship. No matter how loyal, no matter how dedicated, no Jew could be a citizen. During World War II, when the business of the Holocaust began in earnest, the best a German Jew with a history of distinguished service to the German army in World War I could expect was a first-class train trip to the concentration camps at Treblinka or Sobibor. The most one could hope for after a long career in the German government or industry was a place in the "model concentration camp" of Theresienstadt, where people died slowly of disease and malnourishment, rather than quickly as a result of back-breaking labor, starvation, shootings, beatings, and poison gas, as they did in other camps.

German blood alone did not guarantee citizenship, however. Germans had to prove their loyalty to the Reich. Many Germans lost their citizenship because they dared to challenge the authority of the Nazis. Jehovah's Witnesses, political dissenters, Communists, homosexuals, and others who defied the Nazis also were stripped of their citizenship and sent to prison. Unlike Jews, however, members of these other groups could regain their citizenship by renouncing their views. The Jews could not.

The Law for the Protection of German Blood and German Honor

The Law for the Protection of German Blood and German Honor reflected Hitler's obsession with racial purity. Hitler believed that the supposedly pure blood of Aryan Germans was being poisoned through intermarriage with Jews. Hitler believed that the government had a responsibility to prevent sexual relations between Jews and Aryans. In *Mein Kampf*, Hitler wrote:

> A folkish state must therefore begin by raising marriage from the level of continuous defilement of the race, and give it the consecration of an institution which is called upon to produce images of the Lord and not monstrosities halfway between man and ape.[16]

The Law for the Protection of German Blood and German Honor began by stating that "the purity of German blood is a prerequisite for the continued existence of the German people." According to this preamble, the members of the Reichstag were "inspired by the in-

Theresienstadt

Throughout the Holocaust, the Germans claimed that concentration camps were way stations where Jews were held until they were resettled outside of Germany. To support the lie that Jews were being resettled, not killed, the Nazis founded the Theresienstadt concentration camp. The Germans invited inspectors from the Red Cross to tour Theresienstadt, where the detainees appeared to be treated humanely.

Most of the occupants of the Theresienstadt camp were defined under the Nuremberg Laws as partial Jews. Disabled Jewish veterans and Jews who held high positions in German society before the Nuremberg Laws were enacted also were sent to the model camp.

Although it lacked much of the brutality of other camps, Theresienstadt was not a safe haven. According to historian Paul Johnson, of the 141,184 Jews who were sent to the camp, only 16,832 were still alive when it was liberated on May 9, 1945.

flexible will to ensure the existence of the German nation for all times." Believing that racial purity was necessary to achieve this goal, the legislators continued, "the Reichstag has unanimously adopted the following law." The law that followed this preamble banned marriage between non-Aryans and "subjects of German or kindred blood."[17] If an outlawed couple chose to marry anyway, their union would not be accepted as valid by the state, even if it took place in a country where the marriage was legal.

The Law for the Protection of German Blood and German Honor also banned any sexual relationship between non-Aryans and Germans outside of marriage. This portion of the law merely put in writing practices that were commonly in effect. In the 1930s, relatively few Germans had sexual relations outside of marriage; most of those who did were young people who were already engaged. Because of social pressure, few non-Aryans looked outside their communities for mates, and most Aryans would have nothing to do with the non-Aryan minorities. The Nazis were not willing to leave the purity of the Aryan race and the "existence of the German nation" to matters of prejudice, however. They made sex between races a crime.

Although the term "non-Aryan" is often used interchangeably with Jew, the Jews were not the only people the Nazis classified as non-Aryan. The Nazis classified the Gypsies in the same way and subject

Under the Law for the Protection of German Blood and German Honor, even the most private family relationships came under the eye of the Nazi police state.

them to the same treatment as the Jews. As Germany conquered its neighbors to the east, the Nazis also treated people of Slavic origin as non-Aryans.

The Law for the Protection of German Blood and German Honor was not retroactive, that is, it did not apply to marriages that took place before the law was passed. Despite the taboos against interfaith marriages in Germany, many Christian Germans had married Jews prior to the advent of the Nazi state. Those marriages proved to be a thorn in the side of the Nazis. Many Jews were protected from deportation by their Aryan spouse. When a group of Jewish men in Berlin was rounded up by the Gestapo, or secret police, and held pending transfer to a concentration camp, their German wives protested outside, shouting for the return of their husbands. Surprisingly, the men were released.

At the end of the Law for the Protection of German Blood and German Honor, the drafters tacked on the first piece of legislation they had written, the statute forbidding Jews from flying the German flag. Again showing Nazi support for Zionist aims, the law stated that, while Jews could not display the swastika, they were allowed to display "the Jewish colors"—the blue and white Star of David. According to the drafters of the law, "The exercise of this right enjoys the protection of the state." [18]

A Legislative Nightmare

Many marriages between Jews and Germans prior to the Nuremberg Laws produced children, the existence of whom posed one of the most difficult problems the Nazis faced in their efforts to remove Jews from German society and ultimately from the face of Europe.

The issue first came up during those frantic hours when the Nuremberg Laws were originally drafted. Frick, Pfundtner, Stuckart, and Lösener proposed that these people, called *Mischlinge* (singular, *Mischling*) in Nazi terminology, be grouped into different categories. In the urgency of the drafting of the Nuremberg Laws, the framers realized that the issue of people of mixed heritage was too complicated to address at that time. They returned to it two months later to determine the various degrees of *Mischlinge*.

On November 14, 1935, Frick's Ministry of the Interior issued a decree that more exactly defined *Mischlinge*. According to the new decree, people with three or four Jewish grandparents were classified as full Jews. People with "mixed blood" were grouped into two categories: *Mischlinge* First Degree and *Mischlinge* Second Degree:

Age provided no protection from the Nuremberg Laws and their consequences. Here, German soldiers round up Jewish children who will be sent to a concentration camp.

> A Jewish "*Mischlinge*" is anyone who is descended from one or two grandparents—the number of grandparents determined one's "degree"—who are fully Jewish as regards race. . . . A grandparent is deemed fully Jewish without further ado, if he has belonged to the Jewish religious community.[19]

The second sentence had serious consequences for the descendants of Aryans who had converted to Judaism. The law labeled grandparents who were of "Aryan blood" but who had converted to Judaism as Jewish.

Other provisions of this supplementary decree also labeled people Jews who might, looking purely at their family lineage, be labeled *Mischlinge*:

> Also deemed a Jew is a Jewish Mischlinge subject who is de scended from two fully Jewish grandparents and a. who b longed to the Jewish religious community when the law issued or has subsequently been admitted to it; b. wh married to a Jew when the law was issued or has subse

married one; c. who is the offspring of a marriage concluded by a Jew . . . after the Law for the Protection of German Blood and German Honor of September 15, 1935 took effect; d. who is the offspring of extramarital intercourse with a Jew . . . and will have been born out of wedlock after July 31, 1936.[20]

To make sure it was clear to everyone within the Reich who was a Jew or *Mischling,* the Nazis printed and distributed easy-to-understand charts. Jews were represented as black figures, *Mischlinge* were gray, and Aryans were white. The charts also showed which groups were forbidden

Judenrat

Although the Nuremberg Laws declared the circumstances that qualified one as a Jew, the Germans needed a source of information to find out the racial heritage of many people. To find out who was affiliated with the Jewish community, and to facilitate the uses to which they would turn it, the Nazis created the Jewish Councils, or *Judenrat.* These were diverse groups. In some communities, leading citizens took seats on the *Judenrat;* in others a rabbi selected the delegates. In Vilna, where no one volunteered to serve, people drew lots and the council was chosen by sheer chance. In *Never to Forget: The Jews of the Holocaust,* Milton Meltzer explains just how difficult it was to serve on a *Judenrat.* "Its functions were typically dual and opposite: to take charge of survival—health, welfare, supplies; and to take charge of destruction—registration, records, police."

The Jewish Councils in most cases tried to mitigate the harshness of Nazi rule, but were often forced into impossible situations. For example, the Warsaw *Judenrat* organized forced labor squads that performed work dictated by the Nazis. As heartless as this sounds, at least people knew when they had to report for work and the sick and old could be protected. This was a great improvement over the original Nazi system of organizing labor: They simply seized whomever they happened to see on the street.

Different councils tried different strategies for working with the Germans. Ephraim Barash, the head of the *Judenrat* in Bialystock, tried to save the Jews in his ghetto by convincing the Nazi leaders the Jews were valuable workers who could support the war needs. His efforts were unsuccessful. The Nazi's first priority was to kill every Jew ey could. In the Iwaniska ghetto, *Judenrat* head Chaim Rabinowicz se a different path; he helped more than three hundred young le who were strong and willing to fight escape the ghetto and join n units living in the region's forests.

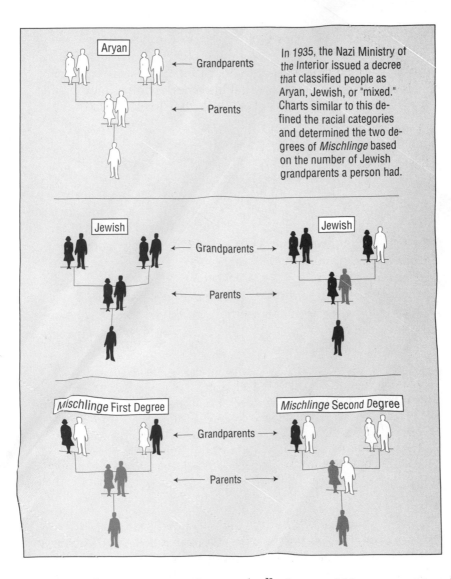

In 1935, the Nazi Ministry of the Interior issued a decree that classified people as Aryan, Jewish, or "mixed." Charts similar to this defined the racial categories and determined the two degrees of *Mischlinge* based on the number of Jewish grandparents a person had.

to marry. Of course, Jews and Aryans (called *Deutschblütigem* in Nazi terminology) could not marry, but neither could a *Mischling*, Second Degree (having only one Jewish grandparent) marry a Jew or another *Mischling*, Second Degree. In the Nazi mindset, it was important to p̶ any situation in which the Jewish bloodline might be strengthen̶

Although this supplementary decree might have appeare̶ closed the issue, it did not. A chronicle of the development̶ state maintains that the arguments over who was a Jew cont̶ out the war. It seems that certain segments of the Nazi̶ wanted to make sure that as many people as possible ̶ in the camps. The Nuremberg Laws made certain ̶

The Roots of Hatred

The Nuremberg Laws were unique to Germany, but anti-Semitism was not. A pessimistic look at the history of Jewish people would seem to indicate that wherever there are Jews, there is hatred for Jews. Like a weed, anti-Jewish sentiment sprouts up throughout history. Although it grew from the same roots as traditional anti-Jewish sentiment, Nazism's grafting of race onto the weed of Jewish hatred made it bear sharp and deadly thorns that first cut Jews out of the national life of Germany and ultimately sent them to their deaths in the gas chambers.

How could Hitler and other Germans come to see Jews as creatures so evil that even infants were deserving of death? The answer lies partly in the development of the Christian Church and partly in economic and social realities.

The Earliest Accusations

The roots of traditional anti-Semitism can be traced to the very natural rivalry between differing religions for adherents and power. Although Christianity began as a small sect within Judaism, by the fourth century it had become the official religion of the Roman Empire. The leaders of the Christian churches used this newfound power to put their enmity for the Jews, who failed to recognize Christian teachings as truth, into practice. Assaults on Jews had a strategic purpose as well. The violence made Judaism a less attractive choice for pagans who were rapidly adopting monotheistic beliefs. The conflict between Christians and Jews took many forms: anti-Jewish laws, false accusations, forced conversions, pogroms, disputations, and expulsions.

Of all the charges Christian leaders leveled against the Jews, none proved more lasting and more deadly than the charge of deicide, the killing of a god. Drawing on biblical sources, church fathers called the killers of Jesus. This teaching ignores the facts that the Jews me were under the control of the Romans, who ordered and the crucifixion of Jesus. Nevertheless, the Jew as Christ- one of the most deeply held beliefs of most Christians, s reason for Christians to persecute Jew.

of years following the rise of the Christian Church usands of anti-Jewish decrees. At different times es, Jews were forbidden to testify in courts, hold certain civil and military posts, and build synagogues, and were barred from observing certain Jewish practices. For example, Justinian I, emperor of the Eastern Roman Empire (527 to 565), issued an edict stating that Passover could be celebrated in a given year only if it came after Easter. In 681, the Sixth Ecumenical Council, a gathering of leaders of the Catholic Church, forbade Christians from seeking treatment from Jewish doctors.

Jews were subjected to special taxes, forced to live in certain parts of cities called ghettos, and made to wear ridiculous clothing and badges. All of these symbols were designed to show that because the people who rejected Jesus lived in such horrible circumstances Jesus and his church were clearly triumphant.

The most lasting and damaging of the charges made against the Jews was that they had murdered Jesus Christ, the messiah of the Christian religion.

Hitler never failed to capitalize on the foundation the Christian churches had laid. In *Mein Kampf* he wrote:

> Two worlds face one another—the men of God and the men of Satan. The Jew is the anti-man, the creature of another god. He must have come from another root of the human race. I set the Aryan and the Jew over and against each other.[21]

Blood Libels

The last fifteen hundred years contain a long record of false accusations leveled against Jews, usually with disastrous results. Two accusations were common: The first was that Jews murdered Christians to use their blood for medicinal purposes or in the preparation of *matzoh,* the unleavened bread that Jews eat during the festival of Passover. The second accusation was that Jews stole the Communion wafer, a symbol of Christ's body, and destroyed it in order to reenact the death of Jesus.

At times, the church teachings that labeled the Jews evil burst into spontaneous mob violence, or, as it came in time to be known among the Jews, pogroms. Some of the bloodiest pogroms occurred during the Crusades, the wars waged between Christians and Muslims for control of Jerusalem and the Holy Land. Some crusaders could not wait to reach Jerusalem to attack the infidels, or nonbelievers. Instead, they attacked Jewish communities that lay in their path. One Jewish observer wrote:

> And when they passed through towns in which Jews were dwelling they said to one another, "Behold we are going to avenge ourselves against the Ishmaelites, and here there are Jews dwelling in our midst whose fathers killed and crucified Jesus. Let us destroy them and obliterate the name of Israel, or let them be like us and acknowledge Jesus as the Messiah."[22]

In the course of the First Crusade, more than twelve thousand died in the Rhineland region of Europe alone.

Not all Christian assaults on Judaism resulted in death. At times, the church was able to force secular authorities to "solve" their "Jewish problems" by expelling their Jewish populations. The most traumatic of these was the Spanish Expulsion of 1492. Spain had been home to a flourishing Jewish community that came to a sudden end when two hundred thousand Jews were forced to leave the country. This long history of violence against Jews created a firm foundation for the passage of the Nuremberg Laws. Hitler and other Nazis did not envision their persecution of Jews as something new, but rather as

As the Christian Crusaders traveled to the Holy Land (now Israel) to battle the Muslim "infidels," they often stopped along the way to massacre Jews, whom they also considered nonbelievers.

an extension of the past. They did not call their campaign against the Jews the "first solution," but rather the "final solution." It was meant to conclude a movement begun centuries earlier.

Even though the power of the Christian churches had waned considerably by the 1930s, the anti-Semitism of the Nazis drew upon the wellspring of anti-Jewish feeling among Christians. Hitler placed Nazi anti-Semitism firmly within the Christian tradition. He wrote in *Mein Kampf*:

> Hence today I believe that I am acting in accordance with the will of the Almighty Creator: by defending myself against the Jew, I am fighting for the work of the Lord.[23]

All About Money

The second root of anti-Semitism revolved around economic realities. Even anti-Jewish actions undertaken for religious reasons often h economic underpinnings. For example, in the twelfth century, Eugenius III announced in a papal bull, or decree, that partic in the Second Crusade would not have to repay debts owed Other debts to Jews were settled by accusing a Jew of ritu or killing him in the course of a pogrom.

Of all the economic realities that led to hostility bet Christians, none was more pervasive or more dama the practice of lending money at interest. The Ca bade Christians from usury. During the last fif

Jews in most of Europe were forbidden from owning land and forced into a limited number of occupations, mostly those Christians did not want. As a result, many Jews went into the business of lending money.

Barred from other professions, many Jews became moneylenders. They, like this thirteenth-century moneylender, were perceived as getting rich at the expense of their Christian neighbors.

Hostility arose when the borrowers felt the rate of interest charged was exorbitant or when failure to repay a debt resulted in foreclosure. The link between economic tensions and anti-Semitism was always strong.

As Germany and the rest of Europe entered the industrial age, businessmen and traders—professions Jews flocked to since they were blocked from so many other fields—became more important and respected. Jews had the know-how and experience to become merchants and industrialists. They moved into these jobs in large numbers, establishing trading routes in many different countries, building factories, and setting up stores.

Ironically, something that German Jews believed brought them closer to their Gentile neighbors—an emphasis on education and learning—in fact fertilized the growing anti-Jewish feeling in Germany. By placing a value on learning, Jews became statistically over-represented in the universities and in lucrative professions such as medicine and law during the nineteenth and twentieth centuries. Their financial successes and disproportionate representation in the professions caused jealousy among some Christian Germans.

The Nazis capitalized on this jealousy and hatred. Many ordinary Germans supported the Nazis because they sensed the Nazi policies would end the economic rivalry between Christians and Jews. The Nazis did not disappoint their followers. The first organized anti-Jewish actions the Nazis undertook involved money. Not only did the [...]s boycott Jewish-owned stores, but they barred Jews from the [...]ities, the legal system, and the practice of medicine. These [...] created openings for non-Jews in these professions.

[...]f the Fittest

[...]conomics were not the only ingredients the Nazis used [...] anti-Semitism. They added philosophy and science, [...]to the cauldron as well. Much of Nazi race theor[...]

had its origins in the writings of German philosopher Friedrich Nietzsche and a theory that came into vogue at the turn of the century, social Darwinism, also known as eugenics.

Although Nietzsche died long before the rise of the Nazis, his writings were distorted to serve Nazi ideological purposes. From the writings of Nietzsche, the Nazis took the idea that a person could find fulfillment in life not through selfless acts of kindness, as the Bible taught, but by acquiring power through the force of will. According to Nietzche, a person could use his "will to power" to gain a preferred position over the meek and weak. Nietzsche called such a person the *Übermensch,* or superman. Nietzsche's "blond beast," a superman whose purpose in life was to rule over others and who answered to no other rules, became the ideal in the Nazi state. By placing Aryans above the Jews, the Nuremberg Laws turned this ideal into a social reality.

At the same time Nietzsche was writing, Charles Darwin advanced the theory of evolution. Designed to explain the differences between species, the theory of evolution was soon adapted to explain differences in society. This theory, known as social Darwinism, preached that people and societies were engaged in the same "survival of the fittest" that Darwin said controlled the biological evolution of animals. Social Darwinism was used as a rationale for imperialism and racism. The Nazis placed the German Aryans at the top of an evolutionary ladder. They declared themselves to be the fittest group on the planet, and thus destined for domination. The Nuremberg Laws reflected this belief. By placing Aryans above Jews, the laws were not fair in the normal sense, but they reflected what was believed to be the natural order of society.

Eugenics is an offshoot of social Darwinism. The term was coined by Francis Galton, a cousin of Darwin's. Not content to let nature take its course in determining who

Friedrich Nietzsche developed the idea of the Übermensch, *or super man. The Nazis would twist writings to serve their racist*

would survive and thrive, proponents of eugenics suggested t' lective breeding should be used to create a higher race of pe defining differences between Jews and Aryans and forbidd marriage between them, the Nuremberg Laws allowed t' put eugenics into practice.

Blood Laws

To the Nazis, one's "blood" was all-important. Keeping "bad blood" out of Germany took the highest priority, and bringing "good blood" in was equally important. In addition to the Nuremberg Laws and other anti-Jewish regulations, the matter of blood regulation was applied in a variety of situations. In *The War Against the Jews 1933–1945*, Lucy Dawidowicz quotes a speech Heinrich Himmler gave to SS leaders on October 4, 1943, that illustrated the Nazi mindset:

> What happens to a Russian or Czech does not interest me in the slightest. What the nations can offer in the way of good blood of our type we will take, if necessary, by kidnapping their children and raising them here with us. Whether nations live in prosperity or starve to death interests me only insofar as we need them as slaves for our Kultur.

To apply for certain jobs, Germans had to show that their family background was all Aryan. The kind of job determined how far back one had to go. For example, to be an SS officer, a person must be able to show that all relatives back to 1750 had been Aryans. German soldiers stationed in the occupied countries who wished to marry local women were forced to submit photos of the women to their superiors. The women were scrutinized to see if they were of the proper racial type before they could be allowed to marry German men.

These new regulations created a new occupation, the *Sippenforscher*, a person hired to research a person's family background to prove that they met Aryan guidelines.

Family researchers had access to the card files at the German Department for Family Research (Sippenforschung).

The "Other"

When Adolf Hitler declared German Jews to be a different kind of entity than other Germans, very few non-Jews pointed out that Jews had been living in Germany before Germany had even existed. Even Germans who had no enmity for Jews were willing to accept Nazi statements that Jews were unlike them in fundamental ways. For example, Heinrich Paulus called the Jews "aliens who could not understand the German soul." Shortly afterward, a Prussian Jew, Gabriel Reisser, responded:

> Where is the other state, to which we owe loyalty? What other fatherland calls us to its defense? We have not emigrated to Germany, we were born here, and either we are Germans or we are men without a country. There is only one baptism that can consecrate a man to nationality: that is the baptism of blood shed in a common battle for fatherland and freedom.[24]

The mass of Germans were unconvinced by Reisser's protestations, as were some Jews.

Chaim Weizmann, an English Zionist working to establish a Jewish state in Palestine, understood this fact very well. In December 1914 he was meeting with Arthur J. Balfour, the British foreign secretary. They talked about a comment made by a woman named Cosima Wagner, who said that Jews were "taking over German culture, science, and industry." Weizmann responded that

Chaim Weizmann recognized that even assimilated German Jews were not fully accepted as citizens of their country.

> the essential point which most non-Jews overlook and which forms the very crux of the Jewish tragedy, is that those Jews who are giving their energies and their brains to the Germans are doing it in their capacities as Germans and are enriching Germany and not Jewry, which they are abandoning. . . . They must hide their Judaism in order to be allowed to place their brains and abilities at the disposal of the Germans. They are to no little extent responsible for German greatness. The tragedy of it all is that whereas we do not recognize them as J[ews], Madame Wagner does not recognize them as Germans, so we stand there as the most exploited and misunders[tood] people.[25]

The Jewish contribution to German culture extended not only to the professions and science, but also to the arts. German Jews such as Otto Brahm, a producer who brought the first realistic dramas to the German stage; Max Reinhardt, who introduced Kammerspiel, plays presented in intimate theaters; plus hundreds of other writers, actors, directors, and musicians took German culture to new heights. These contributions were not uniformly lauded among the German populace. Some Germans felt that the Jews had "kidnapped" German culture and changed it into something foreign and unwelcome. There was even a derogatory term for this process, *Kulturbolschewismus*. The Nuremberg Laws were part of a campaign to return the arts and culture to Aryan control.

The Power of Hatred

Nazi anti-Semitism had roots in religion, philosophy, and science, but it was not a movement of ideas only. It was also a movement of emotions—envy, jealousy, and, mainly, hate. Nearly a century before the Nazis came to power, American historian Henry Adams observed that "Politics, as a practice, whatever its professions, has always been the systematic organization of hatreds."[26]

Right-wing German politicians discovered the power of anti-Semitism as a way to organize people into their movements as early as the 1870s and used it as a steady drumbeat to lure followers. The lower middle classes, in particular, who felt their social standing was in danger, were the first groups to whom the Nazis appealed for support.

Adolf Hitler made no effort to hide his hate-based agenda. Speaking on August 13, 1920, he laid out his beliefs:

> We are convinced that scientific anti-Semitism, which clearly recognizes the frightful danger that that race represents to our people, can only be our guide; the broad masses, who will always react emotionally, must first be made aware of the Jew as the person who, in daily life, is always pushing and everywhere thrusting himself forward—our task must be to arouse the mass instinct against the Jew, to stir it up and keep it on the boil until it decides to support the movement which is prepared to take the consequences.[27]

he roots of anti-Semitism are present in this single statement:
nd prepared by Christian animosity, a sense of the Jew as
economic jealousy and mistrust. What sets this statement
the anti-Jewish speeches that came before it is a single

Rosenberg

Hitler the ex-corporal, criminal, and rabblerouser managed to bend to his cause men of the aristocracy. One such man was Alfred Rosenberg.

Rosenberg was from a family with German roots that lived in the Baltic city of Reval, which had been associated with Germany in its past, but was part of Russia. Handsome and a good speaker, Rosenberg acted as an intellectual mentor to Hitler, fusing the ideas of nationalism, *Volkism*, race, and anti-Semitism into a unified philosophy.

Rosenberg did his best to make bigotry and myth look like scientific truth. He supervised the founding of the Academy of German Law. The organization provided "data" for Nazi anti-Semitic laws, such as the Nuremberg Laws. Rosenberg's one book, *Der Mythos des 20 Jahrhunderts* (*The Myth of the Twentieth Century*), was a pseudoscientific work designed to support the idea that Germans were representatives of the "Aryan" race and were thus destined for domination.

Perhaps none of Rosenberg's ideas had more disastrous consequences than that of *Lebensraum*. *Lebensraum* is the concept that in order to survive and thrive, a country needs adequate land. Germany's need for *Lebensraum* was used as a justification for the Nazi invasion of its neighbors.

Alfred Rosenberg (right) did not fit the profile of most Nazis; he was a well-educated intellectual. It was he who helped Hitler develop the philosophy of the Nazi Party.

Race Theory

Why was race so important to the Nazis? Alfred Rosenberg, one of the leading racial theorists of the Nazi Party, offered the best explanation when he said, "Race is the outside of the soul."[28]

A central tenet of the Nazi belief system was the idea of the German nation as a *Volk*, or people, based on bloodlines. To belong to the nation

47

individuals had to belong to the *Volk;* no contribution made to the nation could bring one into the *volkist* state if one had the wrong "blood."

The Nazis envisioned a hierarchy of races, with Nordic Aryans at the top. The role of those lower on the hierarchy was to serve their racial masters. To the Nazis, the mythic Nordic Aryan race embodied all that was positive, while the non-Aryans were the creators of everything the Nazis saw as negative in the world.

The *volkist* state, historian Lucy Dawidowicz explains, idealized the peasant, who, by virtue of his Aryan bloodlines and the very earth he worked on, became the epitome of the Germanic man. (This is known as the Blood and Soil doctrine.) These opposites, said Adolf Hitler, were destined to clash. The Nuremberg Laws defined who the fighters would be in a racial war.

The Nuremberg Laws also point out how important the Nazis believed it was that the Aryan race stay pure. Hitler wrote in *Mein Kampf:* "The foreign policy of the *Volkist* state must safeguard the existence on this planet of the race embodied by the State, by creating a healthy, viable, natural relationship between the nation's population and growth on one hand and the quality of its soil on the other."[29]

Euthanasia

The Nazi disregard for human life became evident long before it resulted in the wholesale death of Jews. Gassing—the method the Nazis used to execute Jews and other non-Aryans (primarily Gypsies) in the death camps—had been tested long before it was put to work in what the Nazis called the final solution to the Jewish question. On January 2, 1934, a law was passed that enforced sterilization on people the Nazis called "unfit"—the insane, the retarded, and the handicapped. (After the Nuremberg Laws were passed, the Jewish partners in mixed marriages were often forced to undergo sterilization, as well.)

Doctors were also allowed to kill their incurable patients. The Nazis called these murders "mercy deaths." Many of the people who designed, built, and operated the gas chambers at Treblinka, Sobibor, Belzec, and the other extermination camps worked on a project code-named T-4. Between December 1939 and August 1941, between sixty thousand and one hundred thousand handicapped and ill Germans were killed by carbon monoxide gassing and lethal injection in project T-4. The killings finally stopped when the Vatican and German church leaders protested.

The Nazi notions of blood and race made anti-Semitism more dangerous than it had ever been in the past. Prior to the advent of the Nazis and the passage of the Nuremberg Laws, Jews could always opt out of their group by being baptized into the Christian faith. Nazi racial doctrines slammed that door shut. One was born into one's race, a fact, according to the Nazis, that sealed both one's character and one's ultimate fate in a *volkist* state. As Hitler wrote in *Mein Kampf:* "The racial question gives the key not only to world history, but to all human culture."[30]

Nazi anti-Semitism was sure to bring harm to a certain amount of German Jews, but the movement might not have grown to the extent it did were it not for two factors: the outcome of World War I and policies of the German government that followed the war.

World War I

World War I began as a disagreement between two countries—Austria and Russia—over Serbia. What started as a two-state conflict quickly grew into a war that engulfed much of the world. World War I was fought with horribly devastating modern weapons.

When the war ended in 1918, every government involved was deeply in debt. Estimates of the cost of the war reach $90 billion in today's dollars. The victorious powers, which included England, France, and the United States, decided that the losing countries would have to pay for the cost of the war. Since Germany had been one of the main aggressors, most of the debt fell to her. In the Treaty of Versailles, the victors specified a list of crippling punishments that the vanquished Germany would have to endure. War reparations in the amount of $32 billion—payable in currency or goods—were assessed.

Germany was also forced to cede land to Belgium, Czechoslovakia, Denmark, France, Lithuania, and Poland. All of its colonies were taken away. In just a few short years, Germany had gone from being a great power to an impoverished, embarrassed country, and most Germans wanted an explanation. The government avoided blame. The emperor, William II, abdicated and went to the Netherlands. The army was unwilling to concede that poor strategies and logistics had doomed the military effort. The Jews seemed an easy scapegoat, and so Germany's defeat in the war was put down to Jewish treachery.

Things continued to get worse for Germany. The punishments set out in the Treaty of Versailles were far too harsh; there was simply no way Germany could pay back $32 billion. In 1922, Germany missed deadlines on shipments of coal it was supposed to make to help pay off its reparations. France and Belgium responded by occupying the Ruhr Valley, the part of Germany with the largest coal and iron deposits

The Treaty of Versailles was signed at this palace in France. The crushing conditions forced upon Germany by the treaty laid the groundwork for World War II.

Germany responded by refusing to make any more reparations payments at all. This move started an economic panic in Germany. German money became almost worthless. People needed bricks of bills just to buy a loaf of bread. Inflation, an overall rise in the cost of goods and services, went out of control. At one point, inflation was so bad that some German workers were paid each hour and given breaks to run out and do their shopping before the value of the money went even lower. Now more than ever, some Germans needed a scapegoat to blame their problems on, and none was easier than the Jews, who were already perceived as outsiders.

Weimar

The government that came to power in postwar Germany was known as the Weimar Republic. When William II abdicated, the country was in political turmoil. With some meddling from the victorious powers, the government that developed was a democratic republic, an unusual and uncomfortable form of government for a country accustomed to authoritarian leadership. The Weimar Republic was incapable of dealing with the challenges it would face from the Nazis.

Weimar had a parliamentary system, somewhat like the one in modern-day England and Israel. Its form of government gave power small fringe groups like the Nazis. Since the larger parties lacked majorities they needed to pass laws, they had to convince smaller groups to side with them. Once the Nazis managed a political foothold, they used their power well as they built the support they needed to win more seats.

As early as 1924, the Nazis had banded together with other political groups that had similar ideas and won thirty-two seats in the Reichstag. The Weimar Republic simply was not prepared to deal with a group that began its plan to overthrow the state by becoming part of the state.

Wilhelm Frick, one of the central architects of the Nuremberg Laws, held one of those seats. He did not try to hide the Nazi ideals. He introduced two bills (both of which were defeated) that would have made it illegal for Jews to marry non-Jews and would have dismissed Jews from all civil service jobs.

At the same time that anti-Semitic political parties were becoming more powerful, the trickle of anti-Jewish writing that had always been present in Germany grew to a flood. Much of it discussed the supposed Jewish plots that had caused Germany to lose the war and suffer financial ruin. Some anti-Semitic writers brought out the same false allegations that had been made against Jews for centuries: They killed Christian children to make *matzoh* and poisoned wells. Newspapers like *Der Stürmer*, published by Nazi extremist Julius Streicher, added pornography into the mix, printing allegations that Jewish men raped German women.

Here again, the government's basic makeup was unsuited to dealing with the threat this hate speech posed to society. While it was positive that Weimar gave citizens freedoms and opportunities they had lacked before, newspapers like *Der Stürmer* took advantage of the freedom of the press to spew an ever-more violent stream of anti-Semitic writings.

Runaway inflation brought on by the economic terms of the Treaty of Versailles meant that this 500 million mark note printed in 1923 was worth almost nothing.

German schoolbooks of the 1930s used cartoons to promote the idea that Jews were evil and posed a danger to Aryan women and children.

The Weimar government also had no way of dealing with the thousands of soldiers who returned from the front, inured to violence and now without any other employment options due to the economic crisis brought on by the Treaty of Versailles. The Nazis found their most able street fighters among these disenfranchised young men.

The Nazis used the worsening economic situation; people's apprehension about the political and cultural situation in Germany; and the almost unchecked freedom of the press to further inflame anti-Semitic feelings that had always been present in German society.

Just as Hitler mutated anti-Semitic sentiment into the racial hatred that made the Nuremberg Laws possible (and in the minds of their creators and enforcers, necessary), the situation in the years between world wars allowed the Nazis to blossom from fringe group to sole controller of the state.

Unwilling to adapt to the changes involved in changing from the authoritarian monarchy of the kaisers to the more democratic government of the Weimar Republic, the Germans, for the most part, welcomed a party that claimed it would restore calm and legal order. The German demand for lawfulness, unfortunately, was answered by legislation such as the Nuremberg Laws.

CHAPTER 4 Consequences

The Nazis promised to bring law and order to Germany, but they only half-succeeded. They brought law, but not order. In fact, some Nazi laws, especially the Nuremberg Laws, brought about disorder—riots, beatings, and eventually mass death.

Few Germans could foresee where the Nuremberg Laws would lead their nation. From a historical perspective, however, the Nuremberg Laws can clearly be seen as a bridge spanning the chasm between relegating a group of people to a second-class status and packing them in freight trains like cattle and sending them off to be murdered in one of the *Vernichtungslagern,* extermination camps.

There are three basic ways in which the Nuremberg Laws made it possible for Germany to murder millions of Jews. They removed any hope of protection from the state or any recourse to authority. They forbade Jews from forming bonds that might tie them to German citizens who would have the ability to protest and perhaps protect them. Finally, and most ominously, they defined who—when the cattle cars were loaded—would stay and who would go.

Once the Nuremberg Laws stripped away their legal protections, it was easier to round up Jews, like these Polish Jews in the Warsaw ghetto, and deport them to the concentration camps.

Jewish Reaction

Germany's Jews reacted to the laws that defined their status in the Nazi state in two basic ways. Some Jews believed, as historian Yehuda Bauer puts it, "The Nuremberg Laws seemed to guarantee at least life and limb if not spirit."[31] With the passage of the laws, adherents of this position believed, Jews had a clearly defined role in German society. Their social relations were normalized. These Jews saw the Nuremberg Laws as marking the end of an era of changing rules and regulations, when the status of Jews in Germany was as stable as quicksand. At last, it seemed that the Jewish community that had lived in Germany for so many hundreds of years could stay there, albeit under restrictions they had not dealt with since the previous century.

Some Jews perceived the smashing of shop windows in Berlin as divine punishment for sins. Others saw it as a clear notice that Jews should leave Germany.

The Jews were not alone in this belief. Many Nazis shared this view. Historian Eugene Davidson maintains that Wilhelm Frick "thought the Nuremberg Laws not only essential for Germany but good for the Jews. They gave the Jews legal status within the German state."[32]

Some Jews looked to their faith for guidance in how to react to the Nuremberg Laws. Ezra Ben Gershom writes of his father, a rabbi, who viewed the laws as a blessing:

Father saw the guiding hand of God even in the Nuremberg Race Laws. As he saw it, the anti-Jewish legislation of the Third Reich corresponded exactly to the laws of the *Torah* that the German Jews had so often transgressed. Jews opened for business on the Sabbath; hence the fact that the first general boycott of Jewish shops fell on a Sabbath. They married people of other faiths; hence the Nuremberg Race Laws.[33]

Ben Gershom's father was most saddened that the laws penalized their German maid, who had worked for the family for many years. The provision of the Nuremberg Laws that forbade German women under the age of forty-five from working for Jews forced their maid to leave their employment.

54

Other Jews were less sanguine about the Nuremberg Laws. They refused to believe the words of leaders who told them that the fanaticism of Hitler and the Nazi Party could not survive in a civilized country like Germany. For a large portion of Germany's Jews, the Nuremberg Laws served as a clear, unmistakable notice: It was time to leave. What they saw—what Frick and many Jews failed to see clearly—was that the Nuremberg Laws placed the Jews squarely outside the protection of the state, denying them any recourse under the law for whatever assault might come next.

German Reaction

That there would be further assaults should not have been questioned. Hitler himself had said as much. Introducing the laws before the Reichstag, the führer said they were "an attempt to regulate by law a problem that in the event of repeated failure, would have to be transferred to the National Socialist law for final solution."[34] In time, the phrase "final solution" became a Nazi code phrase for the Holocaust.

For many Germans, the Reich Citizenship Law fulfilled what they had been working toward for decades: the disenfranchisement of Germany's Jews. One Nazi official commented after the laws were published, "It will henceforth and for all time be impossible for the Jews to mix with the German people and to meddle in the political, economic, and cultural management of the Reich."[35] Men like Frick were satisfied that the years of struggle and sacrifice they had made for the party culminated in the passage of the Nuremberg Laws. Indeed, this was Frick's moment of greatest influence. As the years wore on, he would lose almost all of his power to younger, more ruthless Nazis.

World Reaction

The Nuremberg Laws did not go unnoticed by the rest of the world. Despite the fact many nations harbored latent anti-Semitism, many foreign leaders condemned the Nuremberg Laws. Negative reaction to the laws forced the Nazis to retreat from the strong anti-Jewish rhetoric and actions taken in the fall of 1935 in the aftermath of the laws. Berlin was slated to be the site of the 1936 Olympic games, but negative feelings about the Nuremberg Laws led many representatives of the foreign press to call for a change of location. As a result, many anti-Semitic signs were removed in Germany and Jewish sport teams were once again allowed to train.

People of No Land

Of the three Nuremberg Laws, the Reich Citizenship Law had the most direct and immediate consequences. From the time they gained power in 1933 until the end of World War II, the Nazis constructed a grillwork of laws and decrees that herded the once-successful and assimilated German-Jewish community into an economic, social, and

The Star of David on this streetcar indicates that only Jews could ride it.

ultimately physical ghetto. The Nazis set up prohibitions that dictated what work Jews could do, what foods they could buy, what modes of transportation they could use, what they could do in their leisure time, what kind of education they could get, and even what names they could have. (All German Jews had to take the name Israel or Sara beginning in 1938.) The Reich Citizenship Law helped make these actions possible.

The Reich Citizenship Law stripped millions of people of even the most meager rights. As the Nazi agenda turned from humiliation and oppression to genocide, the Reich Citizenship Law determined who would die and who would not.

Unlike the other two parts of the Nuremberg Laws, the Reich Citizenship Law was applied to all Jews, regardless of whether they were religious Jews with few ties to the German community or ultra-assimilated Jews who had all but left their Jewishness behind. Ezra Ben Gershom describes his brother Leon's girlfriend Lore, who scarcely knew she was Jewish until the Nazis reminded her and her family of their roots:

> Lore belonged to a family that had become completely estranged from the Jewish tradition. She had been unaware of her Jewishness until the Race Laws were introduced. There was something touching in the way she asked about the details of our religious customs and tried to understand the links between the Jewish faith and the persecutions, ancient and modern, suffered by Jewry.[36]

Not all Jews reacted favorably to being reminded of their Jewish status. In the WW II Warsaw ghetto in Poland, the Jewish police force (a group of Jews who worked for the Nazis) was headed by a Jew by the name of Sherinsky, a man who had renounced his faith and converted to Christianity. He was well known for his hatred of Jews and used his position to harass and attack the Jews of the ghetto. Ultimately, he was murdered by the ghetto underground.

The danger of being labeled a Jew was real and immediate after the passage of the Reich Citizenship Law. Daniel Lang, author of *A Backward Look*, describes a lunch with acquaintances in Germany in 1970. His hostess commented on the danger that befell her husband during the course of the war when he was almost classified as a non-Aryan. "Karl had a terrible time in the war," she said. "He was mistaken for a Jew."[37] She went on to explain that because their last name was sometimes considered a Jewish name, a Nazi official suspected he was a Jew passing as an Aryan. For four months, while the Nazis investigated his background, there was constant danger that he would be sent off to a concentration camp.

Oil and Water

Because it sought to regulate intimate personal relationships, the Law for the Protection of German Blood and German Honor was more difficult to enforce. Enforcing the ban on marriages between Aryans and non-Aryans was simple enough, but dealing with couples who had married prior to the law was trickier, especially when many Germans refused to divorce their Jewish spouses.

Leaving aside the theories of race defilement put forth by the Nazis, in a very real sense the prohibition of mixed marriages was crucial to the success of the Nazis' genocidal plans. In addition to the protection such a marriage afforded an individual Jew, it often gave him or her an opportunity to save Jewish relatives. For example, in his book *The Last Jews in Berlin*, author Leonard Gross tells of a Jewish woman

Nazi "racial scientists" thought they could identify suspected Jews by measuring things such as noses and skulls.

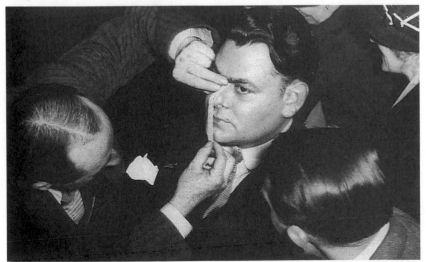

named Anna who was hidden by her brother Max Rosenthal, who was protected from deportation by his marriage to a Christian woman.

The aftermath of the Law for the Protection of German Blood and German Honor created very hard choices for people in mixed marriages. Ruth Thomas, a Jewish woman who survived the war in hiding and whose story is told in *The Last Jews in Berlin*, describes a close friend who was told by the Nazis that if she did not divorce her Jewish husband, she would lose all her property. The friend, like many other Germans in mixed marriages, was torn by her desire to stay with her husband and her fear for his safety.

During World War II, the Nazi leadership in different countries under German control took different approaches to these mixed marriages. For example, in Holland, Jews in mixed marriages were subjected to forced sterilization. The Dutch Nazis were determined to prevent the mixing of blood from one generation to the next.

The seriousness with which Nazis took the matter of "blood" can look ridiculous in hindsight. For example, Leonard Gross tells of a young Jewish boy named Gert Rosenthal who had contracted polio at the age of two (before a vaccine for polio was available). Unlike millions of other victims of this crippling disease, Gert made a complete recovery. Doctors decided to give his blood serum to other polio patients in an effort to help cure them. The Nuremberg Laws brought an end to this experimentation. The Nazis believed that Jewish blood posed a greater threat to Germans than polio did.

A photo shows the aftermath of Kristallnacht. *Because they had defiled German blood, Nazis who raped Jewish women during the* Kristallnacht *pogrom were subject to punishments.*

Not just Jewish blood but any contact with Jews was suspect. In April 1943 an official at the Ministry of Justice wrote a letter to Hitler informing him of a case that had come to the ministry's attention:

> A full Jewess, after the birth of her child, sold her mother's milk to a woman doctor and concealed the fact that she was a Jewess. With this milk, infants of German blood were fed in a clinic. The accused is charged with fraud. The purchasers of the milk have suffered damage, because the milk of a Jewess cannot be considered food for German children.[38]

During *Kristallnacht*, the Night of Broken Glass, November 9, 1938, mobs roamed Germany's streets, destroying synagogues and Jewish businesses and assaulting Jews. Germans who murdered Jews in the course of the night were not punished in any way, but those who raped Jewish women were. This peculiar sense of justice did not reflect a Nazi concern with the well-being of Jewish women. Rather, it revealed the seriousness with which the Nazis guarded the purity of Aryan blood. To the Nazis, the rapists had committed a crime the Nazis believed worse than killing a human being: They had violated the Law for the Protection of German Blood and German Honor. The rapists were immediately expelled from the Nazi Party and turned over to the courts for prosecution.

Mischlinge

Even more than marriages between Germans and Jews, the children of those marriages presented a dilemma to the Nazis throughout the war. The Nazis used all the power of the industrialized, bureaucratic state to build a universe of death, a world in which people—or "units," as the Nazi architects of genocide referred to them—died (at least on paper) at one-minute intervals, in alphabetical order, and of the same cause. This world was the logical result of laws that divided everyone into categories of black and white, us and them, predator and prey. It was also a world singularly ill-prepared to handle the many shades of gray of the *Mischlinge*. In fact, representatives of Frick's Ministry of the Interior argued against declaring any *Mischlinge* to be Jews on the grounds that it would alienate the German parts of mixed families and cause them to resist the Nazis.

Although being qualified as part-Jewish protected a person in theory, it did not always work out that way. Historian Leonard Gross tells the story of a German woman who lost her half-Jewish sons to the Nazis. One son, Ernst, was deported to Buchenwald despite his status as a *Mischling* and the fact that he was married to a Christian woman. He was singled out for punishment because he refused to wear the Star of David badge that was mandated for Jews and part-Jews. Three weeks after he was sent away, his mother received notification that he had died of illness. A second son, Heinz, began a forbidden relationship with a German woman after the Nuremberg Laws were passed. He was picked up by the Gestapo and tortured for two weeks, and died soon after he was released.

The Nazis made exceptions to the *Mischlinge* laws for certain soldiers. For example, Field Marshal Erhard Milch of the Luftwaffe, the German air force, had a Jewish father. When questions arose about Milch's race, Hermann Göring, the head of the Luftwaffe, stepped in. Afraid of losing one of his best officers, Göring had another man, a Christian, declared Milch's biological father.

A memo from the Ministry of the Interior dated October 11, 1935, points out that forty thousand half-Jews are eligible for service in the Wehrmacht, the German army. The memo highlights the contradictions contained in the racial laws. The memo points out that if army veterans who are *Mischlinge* are subjected to anti-Jewish legislation, their condition would be worse than foreigners living in Germany who had fought against the country in World War I.

Even Bernard Lösener, one of the Nazi racial theorists who helped write the Nuremberg Laws, supported treating *Mischlinge* as Germans. A memo he wrote discussed the case of a half-Jew who

Field Marshall Erhard Milch's genealogy was officially changed by the Nazis so that he would not be a Mischling.

had served as an officer in the German army in World War I and who had been twice wounded during the war. Police in the town where this man lived wanted to arrest him because he maintained social contact with Aryans and acted "like a German." Lösener suggested that this man, and other *Mischlinge* like him, be treated like Germans to "silence foreign criticism."[39]

Of all the branches of the armed services, the German navy fought most strongly against the restrictions regarding *Mischlinge*, resisting almost all encroachment from the Nazis. Whenever Nazi bureaucrats would demand that certain *Mischlinge* be discharged from the service, the navy leadership would argue that they be allowed to stay because there was a shortage of trained personnel. At the International Military Tribunal, Admiral Erich Räder

The German Navy tried its best to resist the regulations that barred Mischlinge *from military service.*

testified that only two officers were forced to leave the navy because of their racial status. Even then, the navy helped them find other jobs outside the service.

Even so, *Mischlinge* sailors who were able to stay in the navy still suffered some discrimination. An order of the führer dated August 8, 1940, declared that *Mischlinge* First Degree could be officers in the military because they were needed, but still must be barred from certain privileges. A highly decorated submarine officer was asked at the International Military Tribunal in 1946 if he was a party member. He replied, "I could not belong to the Party because of the Nuremberg Laws."[40]

A Sort of Civil War

The Nuremberg Laws perverted normal relations between people. It gave an individual with a grudge against another person the power to send that person to his or her death. Ruth Thomas, who hid in Berlin during the war, lost her cousin Werner because of his variety of female companionship. One of his girlfriends, upset after the end of their relationship, denounced him for violating the Law for the Protection of German Blood and German Honor when she found out he was having an affair with another Christian woman. Werner spent several years in prison. When the Germans began deporting Jews to the death camps of Poland, he was sent there and perished in a *Vernichtungslager.*

Germans were free to invoke the Nuremberg Laws for the most petty reasons. For example, Otto Stahmer, who served as Göring's lawyer at the International Military Tribunal after the war, arranged the deportation of a Jewish woman named Frau Noak, who had up to that point been protected by her marriage to a Gentile, to the Theresienstadt concentration camp simply because he did not like her living in his building.

Holocaust

Nine days after the passage of the Nuremberg Laws, Hitler called a meeting of his top officials to discuss the issue of the *Mischlinge*. One of the attendees was Bernhard Lösener, the racial theorist who consulted on the laws, who remarked later that he thought the führer spoke very knowledgeably on the subject. During the discussion, Hitler suddenly switched topics from the *Mischlinge* to war plans. Historian Lucy Dawidowicz notes that Lösener thought Hitler was rambling, but there can be no doubt that the two ideas were clearly linked in Hitler's mind. When the war began, the attack on the Jews would begin in earnest.

The years between the passage of the Nuremberg Laws and the horror of genocide were difficult ones for the Jews. The Nazis continued their legislative assault of the Jews, forcing the Jews to sell their businesses to Aryans at extremely low prices, denying Jews the right to own or use telephones, eventually forcing Jews to live in overcrowded ghettos. Jews were forced to wear the identifying Star of David badge at all times, and their ration cards were marked with a letter J. Jews received less food and could only shop at inconvenient hours when the stocks in stores were mostly depleted. Despair overtook the community. By 1938 approximately one hundred German Jews were committing suicide each month.

World War and War on the Jews

As Hitler undoubtedly understood, the outbreak of war would provide the perfect cover for his plans for the Jews. On July 30, 1941, Göring ordered Reinhard Heydrich, the head of the *Sicherheitsdienst* (or SD, the SS Security Service), to "take all preparatory measures . . . required for the final solution of the Jewish question in the European territories under German influence."[41] The preparation yielded three main results: death from starvation and disease, death from overwork (what the Nazis called *Vernichtung durch Arbeit*—elimination through work), and death from gassing or shooting.

The Nazis concentrated Jews in large cities, herding Jews back into the ghettos they had been emancipated from hundreds of years

Warsaw Ghetto Uprising

By the fall of 1942, the population of the Warsaw ghetto had fallen from half a million Jews to just sixty-five thousand due to starvation, disease, and deportations to extermination camps. Facing their own imminent doom, a group of Jewish survivors decided to rebel. They called their group the Jewish Fighting Organization. Led by twenty-four-year-old Mordecai Anielewicz, the group planned to attack the Germans when they came to liquidate the ghetto.

The plans for the uprising had first been formed when mass deportations from the ghetto had begun in 1942, and the Judenrat was forced to deliver six thousand Jews a day to be sent by train to Treblinka. Bernard Goldstein, a representative from the Bund (a Jewish socialist group to which many workers belonged), gave his group's opinion, which Howard Morley Sachar quotes in *The Course of Modern Jewish History:*

> All of us felt that active resistance and obstruction of the deportations was the only possible course. The ghetto had no right to sacrifice 60,000 human beings so that the survivors might continue their slave existence a little longer. Whether we could obtain weapons or not, we owed it to ourselves to resist, with bare hands, if necessary. We could do at least some damage to the Germans by setting fire to the factories and warehouses inside the ghetto. Would it not be better to die in the flames than to wait our inevitable turn to follow the unfortunate 60,000?

The Jews had but a few revolvers, hand grenades, and rifles to wage their fight. With these meager weapons, and whatever rubble from the ghetto they could put to use, the 750 ghetto fighters attacked a German force armed with artillery and tanks.

The Warsaw ghetto uprising began on April 19, 1943, as the Germans moved in in force to crush the ghetto. The rebels killed sixteen Germans and wounded another eighty-five. The Jewish Fighting Organization held out until May 16—longer than some countries with trained, well-armed military forces had resisted the Nazis.

The Warsaw ghetto uprising was heroic but doomed. The few survivors were captured and sent to the death camps.

before. The ghettos made physical the spiritual, social, and economic separation Hitler had worked so hard to build between the Jews and their neighbors and which was clearly outlined in the Nuremberg Laws. In the ghettos, the Jews were easy targets for the Nazi genocidal impulse. The ghettos housed far more people than the area could safely hold. The clearly foreseen and immediate outcome was a high death rate due to infectious diseases such as typhus. Jews were allowed only 800 calories of food per day, far below what an adult needs to stay healthy. Being sent to the ghetto was being sentenced to a death by slow starvation.

In the Warsaw ghetto, Jews ate horses and anything else they could find to stay alive.

German industry benefited tremendously from the Holocaust. The concentration camps served as huge pools of slave labor. Jews were not protected by labor laws, and so they were literally worked until they died. When a Jew died while working in a German factory, no explanation was needed. Factory managers simply ordered a replacement. The work was backbreaking, and no matter how dangerous the conditions, safety equipment was never provided. The prisoners worked in the thinnest of rags no matter how severe the weather. At the Mauthausen camp in Austria, prisoners worked in a quarry, breaking stone with picks and axes. According to Paul Johnson, they then carried the granite blocks up 186 very steep steps. The average life expectancy of a quarry worker upon entering the camp was between six weeks and three months.

Einsatzgruppen

The link between the war and the Holocaust grew stronger as German troops spread throughout Europe. For example, when the German army invaded Russia in the spring of 1941, four mobile killing units followed in its wake. These units, known as *Einsatzgruppen,* were responsible for the deaths of more than eight hundred thousand Jews in occupied Russia. They had a simple but effective mode of operation. They moved into a town, rounded up all the Jews, put them on whatever mode of transportation was available, and moved them to remote areas where mass graves had been dug. The Jews were sent into the pits or forced to stand along their edges and shot down with machine guns. The deadliest "action," as the murders were called, took place near Kiev, at the Babi Yar ravine. In two days—September 29 and 30, 1941—thirty-three thousand Jews were murdered.

The Germans who made up the *Einsatzgruppen* shared Hitler's racial beliefs. One SS officer wrote a letter to a Wehrmacht general about the defenseless men, women, and children he was murdering:

> I thank my lucky stars for having been allowed to see this bastard race close up. . . . Syphilitics, cripples and idiots were typical of the lot. . . . They weren't men, but monkeys in human form. Oh, well, there is only a small percentage left of the 24,000 Jews of Kamentez-Podolsk.[42]

Gas Chambers

The actions of the killing squads were bloody, and traumatizing, and the Nazis took pains to find faster, cleaner, and more efficient ways of murdering Jews, experimenting with carbon monoxide and various toxic gases until German doctors and technicians settled on a chemical called Zyklon-B. In the spring of 1942, a group of extermination camps—Auschwitz, Majdanek, Treblinka, Belzec, Chelmno, and Sobibor—were built in Poland. Auschwitz was capable of killing sixty thousand people in a single day.

In the camps, the process of depersonalization that had begun in 1933 and been codified into the Nuremberg Laws reached its apex. A guard in a concentration camp is reported to have called his dog

Mensch (human being or person). He would encourage the animal to attack prisoners by shouting, "Mensch, go after the dogs."[43]

The "Jewish Question"

The Nuremberg Laws demonstrate the fear the Nazis had of "blood poisoning," and the Holocaust was designed to ensure that there would be no Jewish blood left to mingle with that of Aryans. It is nearly impossible to accurately ascertain exactly how many people the Nazis murdered. Estimates of the Jewish dead range from 4.2 to 6 million. Historian Paul Johnson states that of the 8,861,000 Jews in the parts of Europe that fell under Nazi control, 67 percent, or 5,933,900, died.

In addition to the 6 million Jews who perished, it is estimated that the Nazis killed 15 million Russians, 2 million Poles, another 2 million Greeks and Yugoslavs, and 200,000 Gypsies. Countless more civilians died of the hunger and disease that World War II brought with it.

Conceiving of the Inconceivable

Although there is no doubt that most people were aware that Jews were being murdered, the Germans did their best not to speak of it.

Many Jewish ghettos were liquidated by marching the inhabitants into the woods, shooting them, and burying them in mass graves.

Major Concentration Camps in Europe, 1938–1945

FINLAND

ESTONIA

U.S.S.R.

North Sea

SWEDEN

LATVIA

DENMARK

Baltic Sea

LITHUANIA

EAST PRUSSIA

NETHERLANDS

○ Neuengamme

○ Ravensbrück

□ Treblinka

○ Bergen-Belsen

○ Sachsenhausen

□ Chelmno

POLAND

GERMANY

Majdanek □

□ Sobibor

BELGIUM

○ Buchenwald

○ Theresienstadt

□ Auschwitz

□ Belzec

CZECHOSLOVAKIA

FRANCE

Dachau ○

○ Mauthausen

AUSTRIA

HUNGARY

SWITZERLAND

ROMANIA

ITALY

YUGOSLAVIA

Adriatic Sea

Mediterranean Sea

○ Large-scale labor camps
□ Large-scale extermination camps

Written orders were kept to a minimum, and euphemisms were used to maintain an intellectual distance from the reality of the Holocaust. A letter from an employee of industrial conglomerate IG Farben, who visited Auschwitz and described the effects of starvation and the result of escape attempts, provides a perfect example:

> That the Jewish race is playing a special part here you can well imagine. The diet and treatment of this sort of people is in accordance with our aim. Evidently an increase of weight is hardly ever recorded for them. That bullets start whizzing at the slightest attempt of a "change of air" is also certain, as well as the fact that many have already disappeared as a result of a sunstroke.[44]

Deportation to the death camps of Poland was called "resettlement in the east," mass shootings in ditches were called "special treatment." Rare indeed in its candor is a speech Heinrich Himmler made to leaders of the SS:

> Among ourselves, this once, it shall be uttered quite frankly, but in public we will never speak of it. . . . I am referring to the evacuation of the Jews, the annihilation of the Jewish people. This is one of those things that are easily said. "The Jewish people is going to be annihilated," says every party member. "Sure, it's in our program, elimination of the Jews, annihilation—we'll take care of it." And then they all come

Many concentration camp inmates starved to death as a result of small rations and backbreaking labor.

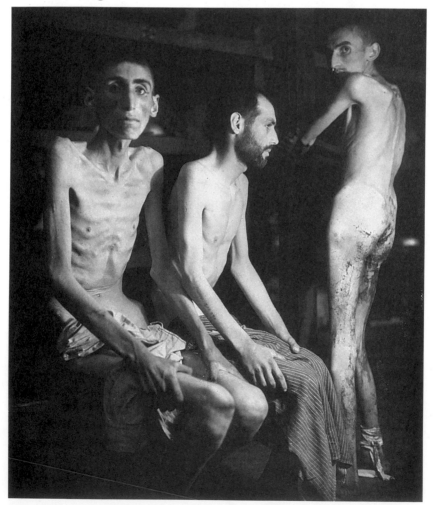

Wannsee Conference

The Wannsee Conference, a confidential gathering of select Nazi officials, was held on January 20, 1942. The main thrust of the conference was to make sure the Jews died as quickly as possible. Starvation and disease in the ghettos were taking too much time. The Nazi leaders agreed to build special camps in which Jews could be killed by the thousands each day.

The results were almost immediate: The next month the Belzec death camp was ready to accept trainloads of Jews. Construction on the Sobibor death camp began in March, and work quickly began to transform Majdanek and Treblinka into death camps, as well.

As late as this conference in 1942, the applications of the Nuremberg Laws had not yet been resolved. The attendees, high-level representatives of the Nazi military and government, spent a portion of the day discussing which categories of *Mischlinge* should be exterminated and which should be allowed to live.

trudging, eighty million worthy Germans, and each one has his one decent Jew. Sure, the others are swine, but this one is an A-1 Jew. Of all those who talk this way, not one has seen it happen, not one has been through it. Most of you must know what it means to see a hundred corpses lie side by side, or five hundred, or a thousand. To have stuck this out and— excepting cases of human weakness—to have kept our integrity, this is what has made us hard. In our history, this is an unwritten and never-to-be-written page of glory.[45]

It is a straightforward matter to record the facts of the Holocaust. Perhaps no other event in modern history has been more thoroughly documented. No matter how many explanations and theories are laid forward, there is no satisfactory answer to the question of how it happened. That human beings pass laws to discriminate against other humans can be proven by a look at the shelves of any law library. That people conspire to kill other people is part of the human condition. But how can a man look at the systematic murder of 6 million people—the young and the old, the sick and the well, men, women, and children— and label it glory? There is no answer.

5 Legalized Hatred

The words "Never again" are written in many books about the Nazi period and emblazoned on many Holocaust memorials. While the world has made strides toward ensuring that the Jews are never again sent to the slaughter, the Nuremberg Laws and their outcome have been mirrored many times in the years since they were passed. Sadly, many people in the world today would gladly return to a day when the Nuremberg Laws were enforced throughout Europe.

Change at the Roots

The Nuremberg Laws did not spring from a vacuum. They grew from centuries of anti-Semitism in Europe. Shocked by the carnage left by the Third Reich, leaders of the Christian Church were faced with the knowledge that the oft-repeated charge of deicide had been instrumental in creating a climate that made the Nuremberg Laws possible. Moreover, religious leaders were forced to acknowledge that they had done little to prevent the violence that followed the disenfranchisement of the Jews. Few people had spoken out against the Nazis. One who did was Father Bernard Lichtenberg of Saint Hedwig's Cathedral in Berlin. The Sunday morning after *Kristallnacht,* Lichtenberg said:

> What took place yesterday, we know; what will be tomorrow, we do not know; but what happens today, that we have witnessed; outside the synagogue is burning, and that, also, is a house of God. . . . In a number of Berlin homes, an anonymous inflammatory rag [pamphlet] is being distributed. It says that any German who, from false sentimentality helps the Jews, commits treason against his own people. Do not let yourself be led astray by such unchristian thoughts, but act according to the dear command of Christ: "Thou shalt love thy neighbor as thyself."[46]

Lichtenberg served two years in prison for making this speech. Upon his release he was seized by the Gestapo and taken to the Dachau concentration camp, where he died.

Lichtenberg was an exception. The majority of priests, pastors, and church leaders either remained silent or encouraged the Nazi regime.

It took many years for the Christian churches to disavow the teachings that helped create a climate in which the Nuremberg Laws could be written and to apologize for their roles in the calamity that anti-Jewish hatred unleashed on Europe. Not until the Second Vatican Council of 1965 did the Roman Catholic Church denounce the charges of deicide, acknowledging that the Romans, rather than the Jews, killed Jesus.

In the 1990s, Catholic bishops in both France and Germany apologized to the Jewish people for the failure of the church to actively oppose the Nazi's anti-Jewish programs. However, the Catholic Church has been unwilling to formally accept a direct link between those teachings and the anti-Jewish legislation and violence of the Nazi era. In a 1998 report on the Holocaust titled "We Remember: A Reflection on the Shoah [Holocaust]," the Catholic Church lay blame

German theologian Martin Luther railed against Jews in the Middle Ages. Almost fifty years after the passage of the Nuremberg Laws, the Lutheran Church turned its back on its founder's anti-Jewish writings.

elsewhere. The report describes the Third Reich as a "neo-pagan regime" rather than the product of a Christian society and claims that "Its anti-Semitism had its roots outside of Christianity and, in pursuing its aims, it did not hesitate to oppose the church and persecute her members also."[47]

Hitler used the words of Martin Luther, the German founder of the Protestant Reformation, to attack the Jews as well. Almost fifty years passed after World War II before the Lutheran Church disavowed Luther's anti-Semitic writings. In 1994 leaders of the church officially condemned such works as *Von die Juden und ihren Lügen* (*On the Jews and Their Lies*). This action might have carried more weight fifty years earlier, however, when organized religion played a larger role in the lives of many people.

Jewish Self-Defense

The situation of the Jewish people was forever changed in 1948 with the founding of the Jewish state. Historians have argued that if Israel had come into being twenty years earlier, the Nuremberg Laws might never have been passed. It is certain that the laws would not have had the impact they did if Israel had existed. First, the notion that Jews

Reparations and Punishment

Some Germans paid with their lives for the genocide that was the main legacy of the Nuremberg Laws. At the International Military Tribunal, twenty-two major war criminals were tried, many for crimes against humanity. Twelve were sentenced to death, three to life in prison, four to long prison terms, and three were acquitted. The trials of Nazis continue to this day, in Germany, in countries that were occupied by the Nazis, and in Israel.

There was also the matter of reparations. The Germans faced stiff financial penalties after World War I; the damage they did in World War II was infinitely greater. The question faced after the war was how to reimburse a person for having been systematically shut out of society. What monetary damage can you assess for declaring someone to not be a citizen? How can you estimate the value of 6 million lives extinguished, and millions of others irrevocably damaged by concentration camp experiences?

The Western powers gave $83 million in Nazi property to Jewish victims. Germany paid restitution to Jews for loss of life, loss of liberty, loss of limb or damage to health, loss of property, and time in which they were forced to wear the star or live in the ghetto. According to historian Paul Johnson, restitution amounted to 5 percent of Germany's budget for twenty-five years and will exceed $30 billion. Restitution payments continue to this day.

The punishment for crimes against humanity was stiff. Back row: Räder—life in prison, Dönitz—ten years in prison. Front row: Ribbentrop—death, Hess—life in prison, Göring—death.

were unlike other people because they did not have a country of their own would have been contradicted by the existence of Israel. (Note that the Gypsies—who suffered an identical fate under the Nazis— also were a people without an ancestral homeland.) Second, Israel would have provided what no other country was willing to provide—an

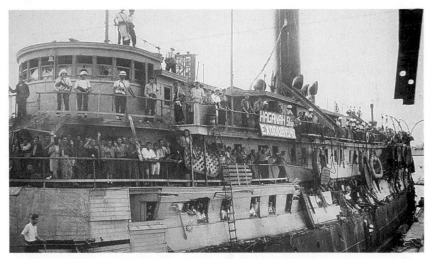

Jewish survivors eager to leave Europe behind took any transportation available out of Europe. Here, the Exodus *lands at Haifa, Palestine, July 18, 1947.*

open port for the thousands who wished to escape the anti-Semitism of the Hitlerites. Third, a Jewish state would have opposed, by foreign policy and popular will, the Nazis and their anti-Jewish laws and actions in whatever way possible.

Today Jewish organizations such as the Anti-Defamation League fight the sort of anti-Semitism that led to the passage of the Nuremberg Laws. Some groups work to lobby their governments for protection for religious freedoms and against discrimination of any sort. Other Jewish groups focus on training their members to defend themselves against physical attacks.

What Has Not Changed

Although strides have been made toward stepping away from the situation that made the Nuremberg Laws possible, some of the same forces that were at work in the 1930s and 1940s are still evident today. Foremost of these is the idea that race is a defining characteristic of a person. This notion ignores the fact that the concept of race is not supported by biological realities. While a black person might be described as someone with dark skin and curly hair, there are many examples of people who are called black who have light skin and straight hair. There are also people who are called white who have dark skin and curly hair.

Racists, like the Nazis, argue that people of different races should not be allowed to marry and have children. They group the children of mixed marriages with the race they do not like, which is an illogical assumption. Nevertheless, racists continue to declare that certain races are more prone to commit crimes, which ignores the role that other factors play in fostering crime. They insist that certain races are smarter than others, which ignores the fact that in the United States some groups get a better education based on the amount of money they have and the area in which they live.

Many politicians are still willing to exploit dislike and fear of other groups to gain support for themselves. A prime example is the effort to cut off government benefits to legal immigrants and to limit immigration into the United States. Since most immigrants today come from places such as Central and South America, Asia, Africa, and the Middle East, these efforts target groups who do not look like the majority of Americans.

Although the situation that led to the passage of the Nuremberg Laws and the ensuing anti-Jewish violence and murder was the product of a unique set of historical circumstances, there have been, unfortunately, parallels in the ensuing years. All that is required for a repeat of the Nuremberg Laws is a few factors: the belief that one group is superior to another and that the survival of the first group depends on subjugating the other, a group with a willingness to act on those beliefs, a group with the power to act, and a population willing to stand idly by while the minority is attacked.

Jim Crow

All of these factors were present in the American South after the Civil War. At least until the 1960s, a large number of southern whites believed blacks were inferior. Because whites held most of the political power in the South, they were able to put those beliefs into action, supported by most whites either overtly or with their silence.

The actions taken against African Americans fell short of the Nazis' all-out war against the Jews, but some of the laws governing blacks were nearly identical to parts of the Nuremberg Laws. For example, all southern states had laws that forbade the intermarriage of blacks and whites. These laws were based on the same kinds of ideas that formed the Law for the Protection of German Blood and German Honor. Many of these laws not only predated the Nuremberg Laws, but they remained in force even after the end of World War II.

In addition, blacks and whites were kept separate in public places. (The laws that enforced the separation were known as Jim Crow laws.) Blacks were not allowed to eat in the same restaurants or stay in the same hotels as whites; there were separate water fountains for blacks; and bathrooms were labeled "Men," "Women," and "Colored." There were even separate hospitals and cemeteries for blacks and whites.

African Americans were also shut out of the political system by restrictive laws. One such law was known as the grandfather clause. It required new voters to prove that their ancestors had registered to vote in a given year, usually a year when blacks could not vote. Some states also required that voters pay a poll tax. Since most blacks were poor, the poll tax prevented many of them from voting. Voters in some states were required to pass literacy tests before they voted. This law reduced the number of black voters, since many blacks had never been given access to education.

The fact that blacks were viewed as inferior and shut out of the political system had deadly effects. White Southerners lynched many African Americans, not because they had committed crimes, but to remind the black community that the whites were in control. Law enforcement officials did little to stop lynchings. In some cases, law enforcement officials allowed blacks

In the American South, public facilities like this water fountain were labeled "Colored" and "White."

accused of crimes to be taken out of jails and murdered by mobs. Many of these actions were instigated by the Ku Klux Klan, which, like the Nazi Party, counted many sheriffs and policemen among its members.

In a striking similarity to the brutal medical experiments that were performed on concentration camp inmates, poor black men in Tuskegee, Alabama, were used in the Tuskegee Study of Untreated Syphilis in the Negro Male. In this experiment, men who had been infected with syphilis (which is easily treated with penicillin), were never told of their condition. Instead, the course of their untreated disease was tracked and documented.

Apartheid

The system that most closely paralleled the Nazi oppression of Jews existed in South Africa from 1948 until the 1990s. This system, known as apartheid (apartness), was designed to keep the white minority of South Africa in a dominant position over the black majority. Like the Nazi system, apartheid was backed by a system of national laws that maintained strict segregation based on race. The goal of apartheid was not to exterminate a certain race, and the South African government did not commit genocide. Nevertheless, life under apartheid strongly resembled the early years of life under the Nuremberg Laws.

Under apartheid, every person in South Africa was placed into a racial category: Whites (who made up 13 percent of the population), Africans (77 percent), Coloureds, or people of mixed heritage (8 percent), and Asians (2 percent). The Whites were declared to be the majority by breaking the Africans up into 10 separate groups, based on language and origin. The Whites claimed that these African groups were as different from one another as they were from the Whites. To support this legal fiction, the government of South Africa set aside certain areas, called homelands, for each of the groups. Four of the homelands were called independent countries, although other countries did not recognize the homelands as such. The Africans were declared to be citizens of a given homeland, rather than of South Africa.

In South Africa before the end of apartheid, access was based on race, as this sign on a beach in Smithtown shows.

Even if they did not live in the homelands, Africans could not be South African citizens. This situation is highly reminiscent of the Reich Citizenship Law, which refused to recognize Jews as German citizens.

Like the Jews, the ethnic groups of South Africa were forced to live in certain areas, much like ghettos. Living conditions in the black townships were horrible, and led to a higher death rate due to disease and improper sanitation. In laws that mirror the anti-Jewish statutes of the Nazi period, access to employment and recreational and other facilities was based on one's racial identity. As the Jews did under the Nazis, blacks were forced to carry special permits. They could not travel into the white areas, where many worked as domestic help such as maids and gardeners, without having a special permit. The law banning marriage between groups lasted much longer than the Law for the Protection of German Blood and German Honor did; it was passed in 1948 and was not reversed until 1985.

As in Nazi Germany and the American South, ethnic hatred led inevitably to violence in South Africa. In the 1980s, the police in South Africa were used to put down efforts by the blacks to gain equality.

The apartheid laws of South Africa created ghettos, like this all-black settlement near Johannesburg.

Thousands of people were detained without a trial and many detainees died in police custody after being tortured. Hundreds more were shot and killed by the military when they participated in rallies to protest apartheid policies.

Not until 1994 did all racial groups in South Africa gain political power. The situation for blacks remains difficult, as employment opportunities are still limited and decades of racism have created a group of people who still believe that blacks are inferior. A body known as the Truth and Reconciliation Commission was formed to investigate the antiblack violence that claimed so many lives in the last years of the apartheid era.

Yugoslavia

The ethnic warfare that has convulsed the Balkan region of Europe provides another example of how ethnic hatred and the use of those feelings by politicians can lead to disastrous consequences. The country of Yugoslavia, which comprised the republics of Serbia, Croatia, Slovenia, Bosnia and Hercegovina, Montenegro, and Macedonia, was a multiethnic society of people of diverse backgrounds and religions. The country began to break up in 1991 when Croatia and Slovenia seceded, followed in 1992 by Bosnia. Some groups maintained that their ethnic identity was more important than where they lived. For example, the Bosnian Serbs gained the support of the Yugoslav military, which was predominantly Serbian, to resist the Bosnian government. The Serbs forced Muslims and Croats—the other two groups that

In the Balkans, war has provided a cover for "ethnic cleansing" and genocide and has resulted in mass graves, like this one containing Muslim victims near the Bosnian village of Nova Kasaba.

make up most of the Bosnian population—to leave Serb-controlled areas of the country. This policy, which was called euphemistically "ethnic cleansing," forced approximately 3 million refugees from their homes. Ethnic cleansing was used as a cover for genocide; there have been mass murders of civilians throughout the Balkans. Concentration camps also sprang up, in which many people died of disease and starvation.

Unlike Nazi anti-Semitism, ethnic cleansing was not enshrined in laws similar to the Nuremberg Laws, nor did the practice affect the millions of people harmed in the Holocaust. Nevertheless, the parallels between the genocide of the Third Reich and the ethnic cleansing of the former Yugoslavia are striking. In fact, German neo-Nazis, modern-day racists who call for a return to the policies of the Third Reich, went to fight alongside the Croat forces, practicing murdering Serbs for the day when they would be able to kill Jews. Ingo Hasselbach, a former East German neo-Nazi leader, called the racial warfare in the former Yugoslavia "a neo-Nazi dream come true."[48]

Unfortunately, although many countries have passed laws that target hate crimes against individuals—crimes based on the victim's race, religion, or sexual orientation—the world, for the most part, turned its back when ethnic hatred erupted into mass murder in the former Yugoslavia. The international community was, as in the case of the Holocaust, slow to react to the ethnic violence.

Art and Gold

More than a half-century after
the passage of the Nuremberg Laws,
the German nation continues to face the
effects of Nazi ideologies. In the same way
that Germany tried to "cleanse" itself by shipping
Jews to Poland, the country sold the "degenerate art"
it looted from Jews to foreign countries. Many of these
works of art were masterpieces by such painters as Claude
Monet and Henri Matisse. Those works are only now beginning to
be returned to the owners or their heirs.

The effort to return stolen art to its original owners has been hampered by falsified sales documents, unwillingness by collectors who paid large sums to relinquish the art they possess, and the fact that in many cases the original owners and their heirs all died under the Nazis. Moreover, with hundreds of thousands of pieces of art in question, the task is huge. Nonetheless, some efforts have succeeded. For example, in the early part of 1998, France returned a painting by Japanese artist Tsuguharu Fujita to the heirs of its original, Jewish owner.

Efforts are also being made to obtain restitution for money deposited in Swiss banks by people killed in the Holocaust. In addition, a great deal of Nazi gold remained in Swiss banks. Some of this gold was seized by the Nazis from people in the concentration camps. Much of it came from the gold fillings in the teeth of people who died in the gas chambers. The value is estimated to be near $8.5 billion in today's dollars.

After years of denials from Swiss banks that they were holding funds deposited by Jews who died in the Holocaust, the Swiss banking industry has begun to make efforts to return money to the heirs of those who perished. Recognizing that in many cases whole families

were wiped out or the few remaining survivors have since passed away, the Swiss banks have also set up a $200-million fund that will provide funds for elderly Jewish Holocaust survivors.

Thousands of gold wedding rings were taken from Jews before they went to the gas chambers. The gold helped finance the German war effort.

Eventually, a Yugoslav war crimes tribunal was formed to punish those responsible for murder, rape, and torture. Included in the list of criminals is Bosnian Serb leader Radovan Karadzic, a psychiatrist who used the ethnic tensions of his country to gain power. He steadfastly maintained that the Serbs, Muslims, and Croats could not possibly live together in a multiethnic state. By waving the banner of ethnicity, he was able to form a group of people who agreed with him and were willing to fight.

Neo-Nazism

Despite the total defeat of the Nazis in World War II and the fact that almost all the party's leaders died or were imprisoned, the Nazi movement is not dead. It lives on in hundreds of small neo-Nazi groups around the world.

Shortly before he committed suicide in his Berlin bunker on April 30, 1945, Hitler made his final statement: "Above all, I bind the leadership and its subordinates to the painful observance of the racial laws and to merciless resistance of the world-poisoner of all nations, international Jewry."[49] It is the racial myths that provided the intellectual framework for the Nuremberg Laws that have proven to be the most enduring part of the Nazi legacy.

Shared Ideals

The *volkist* philosophy of the Nazis has been wholeheartedly embraced by the neo-Nazis, who are all too happy to mix nationalism with racism. Neo-Nazis also support the concept of Blood and Soil; they continue to maintain that it is man's ties with the earth that make him who he is. Today, the neo-Nazi movement often hides its real intent in the guise of ecological activism. Other neo-Nazi groups are active in the antiabortion movement. Like Germans of the Nazi era, they seek to create larger white families; the same people who fight against abortions in public often call, in private, for the sterilization of minorities.

Like the original Nazis, the neo-Nazis use religion to further their arguments. Some call for a return to early Germanic pagan religions. Faiths like Asatru, which worships the old Norse gods such as Odin, Thor, and Freya, are popular with neo-Nazis. (Of course, the vast majority of pagans have no involvement with racist groups.) Neo-Nazis who adhere to Asatru and its related sects claim that these are the true gods of people of their ethnicity and that Christianity, Islam, and Judaism are alien religions that were forced on them. Arnulf Priem, the head of a pagan neo-Nazi group called Wotan's Volk, openly advocates a return of the Nuremberg Laws.

The Ku Klux Klan shares many Nazi ideals, but lacks their power. Police are often required to protect the Klan when it holds rallies, like this one to protest Hispanics moving into a Georgia community.

The World Church of the Creator, another neo-Nazi group, has dispensed with gods altogether and has turned race into religion; the only thing that is important is to do what is best for one's race. Predominantly, this means not marrying or having children with people of other ethnic groups. This organization claims that nonwhites are subhuman. The World Church of the Creator's links to the German Nazis can easily be seen by visiting the group's World Wide Web page on the Internet. Adolf Hitler is portrayed predominantly throughout the site. The group subscribes to the idea that the basis of society is the inevitable struggle between white Aryans and Jews. The struggle for *Lebensraum*—living space—is also central to World Church of the Creator ideology.

Other neo-Nazis choose to bend Christian theology to their own needs. In recent years, a movement known as Christian Identity has become increasingly popular in racist circles. Christian Identity teaches that when the Christian Bible speaks of Israel, it is referring to white people. Christian Identity labels nonwhites subhuman and claims that Jews are descended from the devil. Like other neo-Nazi organizations, adherents to the teachings of Christian Identity stress that white people should not intermarry with other groups. Although they lack the political power to pass legislation such as the Law for the Protection of German Blood and German Honor, they seek to convince people to adhere to the same rules voluntarily.

Political Anti-Semitism

Groups such as the National Alliance, a self-proclaimed Aryan organization, reiterate the claims of the Nazis that Jews compete unfairly in business. They maintain that Jews control world financial markets and the mass media. They state that if they come to power, they will, as the Nazis did in Germany, block Jews from owning businesses and working in any of the media. Like the Nazis, these groups stress that Jews and nonwhites are fundamentally different from whites. They also claim that there is a racial hierarchy, with whites holding the top spot. Neo-Nazis train for a day when they will be back in power and will be able to put their ideals into practice. In the meantime, they conduct war games and play computer simulation games, including one called Concentration Camp Manager.

American Neo-Nazis

A strange relationship exists between the neo-Nazi movements in the United States and Germany. The American neo-Nazis idealize all things German. A leading American neo-Nazi, Gerhard (born Gary) Lauck goes so far as to speak English with a German accent. At the same time, most printed material distributed in Germany comes from the United States. Germany has strict laws against hate speech,

Modern-day racists borrow symbols from history. The neo-Nazi with a swastika shirt and a Hitler-style mustache stands next to a man holding a Confederate flag.

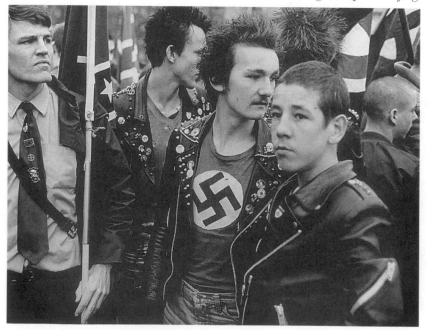

while the American Constitution guarantees the rights to free speech and freedom of the press, which includes the freedom to publish neo-Nazi pamphlets, stickers, newspapers, and other materials. According to the former East German neo-Nazi leader Ingo Hasselbach, to Lauck, "Germany was the only Fatherland and the 'Jew-nited States' was useful only because it had no restrictions on weapons and political speech."[50] Lauck, who is sometimes called the Farmbelt Führer and wears a Hitler-style mustache, once headed a group that printed posters, neo-Nazi propaganda, and a newspaper called *Battle Cry* (in six languages). Today, Lauck is serving time in a German prison for violating that country's ban on hate speech.

The ties between German and American neo-Nazis are very close; Hasselbach (who ultimately left the movement) explained that he traded strategies and ideas with American Tom Metzger (the head of White Aryan Resistance, a group that was linked to the beating death of an Ethiopian immigrant) and Dennis Mahon of the Ku Klux Klan.

The Neo-Nazi Future

Unfortunately, neo-Nazi groups seem to be gaining popularity. The Southern Poverty Law Center, an organization that tracks hate groups, reports that the neo-Nazi World Church of the Creator was twice its 1996 size in 1997. Another American neo-Nazi group known as the National Alliance also was very successful in recruiting new members, opening a number of new chapters in 1997. The number of people associated with neo-Nazi groups in Germany also continues to climb, despite strict laws against such activity. A report commissioned by the German government indicates that neo-Nazi incidents are on the rise in the German military. One reported incident involved two German army officers who were serving in Bosnia. The two are alleged to have made anti-Semitic insults at Albanian soldiers. People who support the ideals that gave birth to the Nuremberg Laws are willing to stand up for their beliefs. The first International National Socialism Gathering is scheduled to be held in Chile in April 2000.

Politicians continue to find that anti-Semitism can be a powerful organizational tool. In the Russian province of Krasnodar, the governor, Nikolai Kondratenko, made a speech blaming Russia's economic problems on Jews. It is exactly these sentiments that can lead to demands that "Jewish power" be restrained by laws—laws similar to those passed in Nuremberg in 1935.

Appendix

The Nuremberg Laws on Citizenship and Race

In The Holocaust: Selected Documents in Eighteen Volumes, *John Mendelson provides this translation of the Nuremberg Laws.*

The Reich Citizenship Law of September 15, 1935

THE REICHSTAG HAS ADOPTED by unanimous vote the following law which is herewith promulgated.

ARTICLE 1. (1) A subject of the state is one who belongs to the protective union of the German Reich, and who, therefore, has specific obligations to the Reich. (2) The status of subject is to be acquired in accordance with the provisions of the Reich and the state Citizenship Law.

ARTICLE 2. (1) A citizen of the Reich may be only one who is of German or kindred blood, and who, through his behavior, shows that he is both desirous and personally fit to serve loyally the German people and the Reich. (2) The right to citizenship is obtained by the grant of Reich citizenship papers. (3) Only the citizen of the Reich may enjoy full political rights in consonance with the provisions of the laws.

ARTICLE 3. The Reich Minister of the Interior, in conjunction with the Deputy to the *Fuehrer,* will issue the required legal and administrative decrees for the implementation and amplification of this law.

Promulgated: September 16, 1935. In force: September 30, 1935.

Law for the Protection of German Blood and German Honor
September 15, 1935

Thoroughly convinced by the knowledge that the purity of German blood is essential for the further existence of the German people and animated by the inflexible will to safe-guard the German nation for the entire future, the Reichstag has resolved upon the following law unanimously, which is promulgated herewith:

SECTION 1 1. Marriages between Jews and nationals of German or kindred blood are forbidden. Marriages concluded in defiance of this law are void, even if, for the purpose of evading this law, they are concluded abroad. 2. Proceedings for annulment may be initiated only by the Public Prosecutor.

SECTION 2 Relation outside marriage between Jews and nationals of German or kindred blood are forbidden.

SECTION 3 Jews will not be permitted to employ female nationals of German or kindred blood in their households.

SECTION 4 1. Jews are forbidden to hoist the Reich and national flag and to present the colors of the Reich. 2. On the other hand they are permitted to present the Jewish colors. The exercise of this authority is protected by the State.

SECTION 5 1. A person who acts contrary to the prohibition of section 1 will be punished with hard labor. 2. A person who acts contrary to the prohibition of section 2 will be punished with imprisonment or with hard labor. 3. A person who acts contrary to the provisions of section 3 or 4 will be punished with imprisonment up to a year and with a fine or with one of these penalties.

SECTION 6 The Reich Minister of the Interior in agreement with the Deputy of the *Fuehrer* will issue the legal and administrative regulations which are required for the implementation and supplementation of this law.

SECTION 7 The law will become effective on the day after the promulgation, section 3 however only on 1 January, 1936.

Nuremberg, the 15th day of September 1935 at the Reich Party Rally of Freedom.
The Fuehrer and Reich Chancellor Adolf Hitler
The Reich Minister of the Interior Frick
The Reich Minister of Justice Dr. Goertner
The Deputy of the Fuehrer R. Hess

First Supplementary Decree of November 14, 1935

On the basis of Article III of the Reich Citizenship Law of September 15, 1935, the following is hereby decreed:

ARTICLE 1. (1) Until further provisions concerning citizenship papers, all subjects of German or kindred blood who possessed the right to vote in the *Reichstag* elections when the Citizenship Law came into effect, shall, for the present, possess the rights of Reich citizens. The same shall be true of those upon whom the Reich Minister of the Interior, in conjunction with the Deputy to the *Fuehrer,* shall confer citizenship. (2) The Reich Minister of the Interior, in conjunction with the Deputy to the *Fuehrer,* may revoke citizenship.

ARTICLE 2. (1) The provisions of Article I shall apply also to subjects who are of mixed Jewish blood. (2) An individual of mixed Jewish blood is one who is descended from one or two grandparents who, racially, were full Jews, insofar that he is not a Jew according to Section 2 of Article 5. Full-blooded Jewish grandparents are those who belonged to the Jewish religious community.

ARTICLE 3. Only citizens of the Reich, as bearers of full political rights, can exercise the right of voting in political matters, and have the right to hold public office. The Reich Minister of the Interior, or any agency he empowers, can make exceptions during the transition period on the matter of holding public office. The measures do not apply to matters concerning religious organizations.

ARTICLE 4. (1) A Jew cannot be a citizen of the Reich. He cannot exercise the right to vote; he cannot hold public office. (2) Jewish officials will be retired as of December 31, 1935. In the event that such officials served at the front in the World War either for Germany or her allies, they shall receive as pension, until they reach the age limit, the full salary last received, on the basis of which their pension would have been computed. They shall not, however, be promoted according to their seniority in rank. When they reach the age limit, their pension will be computed again, according to the salary last received on which their pension was to be calculated. (3) These provisions do not concern the affairs of religious organizations. (4) The conditions regarding service of teachers in public Jewish schools remains unchanged until the promulgation of new laws on the Jewish school system.

ARTICLE 5. (1) A Jew is an individual who is descended from at least three grandparents who were, racially, full Jews . . . (2) A Jew is also an individual who is descended from two full-Jewish grandparents if: (a) he was a member of the Jewish religious community when this law was issued, or joined the community later; (b) when the law was issued, he was married to a person who was a Jew, or was subsequently married to a Jew; (c) he is the issue from a marriage with a Jew, in the sense of Section I, which was contracted after the coming into effect of the Law for the Protection of German Blood and German Honor of September 15, 1935; (d) he is the issue of an extra-marital relationship with a Jew, in the sense of Section I, and was born out of wedlock after July 31, 1936.

ARTICLE 6. (1) Insofar as there are, in the laws of the Reich or in the decrees of the National Socialist German Workers' Party and its affiliates, certain requirements for the purity of German blood which extend beyond Article 5, the same remain untouched. . . .

ARTICLE 7. The *Fuehrer* and Chancellor of the Reich is empowered to release anyone from the provisions of these administrative decrees.

Source Notes

Chapter 1: Denial and Adaptation

1. Quoted in Lucy S. Dawidowicz, *The War Against the Jews 1933–1945*. New York: Holt, Rinehart, and Winston, 1975, p. 4.
2. Quoted in Paul Johnson, *A History of the Jews*. New York: Harper & Row, 1987, p. 472.
3. Quoted in Eugene Davidson, *The Trial of the Germans: Nuremberg 1945–1946*. New York: Macmillan, 1966, p. 76.
4. Quoted in Dawidowicz, *The War Against the Jews*, p. 68.
5. Quoted in Dawidowicz, *The War Against the Jews*, p. 70.
6. Quoted in Howard Morley Sachar, *The Course of Modern Jewish History*. New York: Dell, 1958, pp. 148–49.
7. Quoted in Yehuda Bauer, *A History of the Holocaust*. New York: Franklin Watts,1982, p. 225.

Chapter 2: Putting Prejudice into Action

8. Quoted in Dawidowicz, *The War Against the Jews*, pp. 124–25.
9. Davidson, *The Trial of the Germans*, p. 261.
10. Joseph E. Persico, *Nuremberg: Infamy on Trial*. New York: Penguin Books, 1994, p. 226.
11. Quoted in Davidson, *The Trial of the Germans*, p. 263.
12. Quoted in Sachar, *The Course of Modern Jewish History*, p. 431.
13. Quoted in Persico, *Nuremberg*, p. 271.
14. Quoted in Bauer, *A History of the Holocaust*, pp. 102–103.
15. Quoted in Bauer, *A History of the Holocaust*, pp. 102–103.
16. Quoted in Dawidowicz, *The War Against the Jews*, p. 86.
17. Quoted in Bauer, *A History of the Holocaust*, pp. 103–104.
18. Quoted in Bauer, *A History of the Holocaust*, pp. 103–104.
19. Quoted in Bauer, *A History of the Holocaust*, pp. 103–104.
20. Quoted in Bauer, *A History of the Holocaust*, p. 104.

Chapter 3: The Roots of Hatred

21. Quoted in Dawidowicz, *The War Against the Jews*, p. 27.
22. Quoted in Bezalel Narkiss, ed., *Picture History of the Jewish Civilization*. Jerusalem: Massada, 1978, pp. 114–15.
23. Quoted in Dawidowicz, *The War Against the Jews*, p. 27.
24. Quoted in Sachar, *The Course of Modern Jewish History*, p. 105.
25. Quoted in Johnson, *A History of the Jews*, p. 428.
26. Quoted in Hugh Rawson and Margaret Miner, eds., *The New International Dictionary of Quotations*. New York: NAL Penguin, 1986, p. 272.

27. Quoted in Helmut Krausnik et al., *Anatomy of the SS State.* New York: Walker, 1965, p. 21.

28. Quoted in Davidson, *The Trial of the Germans*, p. 134.

29. Quoted in Dawidowicz, *The War Against the Jews*, p. 120.

30. Quoted in Dawidowicz, *The War Against the Jews*, p. 23.

Chapter 4: Consequences

31. Bauer, *A History of the Holocaust*, p. 280.

32. Davidson, *The Trial of the Germans*, p. 271.

33. Ezra Ben Gershom, *David: Testimony of a Holocaust Survivor.* New York: Berg, 1988, pp. 57–58.

34. Quoted in Sachar, *The Course of Modern Jewish History*, p. 91.

35. Quoted in Milton Meltzer, *Never to Forget: The Jews of the Holocaust.* New York: HarperCollins, 1976, p. 37.

36. Ben Gershom, *David*, p. 195.

37. Daniel Lang, *A Backward Look: Germans Remember.* New York: McGraw-Hill, 1979, p. 86.

38. Quoted in Johnson, *A History of the Jews*, p. 473.

39. Quoted in Davidson, *The Trial of the Germans*, p. 269.

40. Quoted in Davidson, *The Trial of the Germans*, p. 56.

41. Quoted in Sachar, *The Course of Modern Jewish History*, pp. 441–42.

42. Quoted in Sachar, *The Course of Modern Jewish History*, p. 444.

43. Quoted in Davidson, *The Trial of the Germans*, p. 8.

44. Quoted in Johnson, *A History of the Jews*, pp. 491–92.

45. Quoted in Dawidowicz, *The War Against the Jews*, p. 200.

Chapter 5: Legalized Hatred

46. Quoted in Ingo Hasselbach and Tom Reiss, *Führer-Ex; Memoirs of a Former Neo-Nazi.* New York: Random House, 1996, p. 55.

47. "Papal Holocaust Apology Disappoints Jews," *San Diego Union-Tribune*, March 17, 1998, p. A2.

48. Hasselbach and Reiss, *Führer-Ex*, p. 207.

49. Quoted in Sachar, *The Course of Modern Jewish History*, pp. 458–59.

50. Hasselbach and Reiss, *Führer-Ex*, p. 163.

For Further Reading

David A. Altshuler, *Hitler's War Against the Jews: A Young Reader's Version of the War Against the Jews 1933–1945 by Lucy S. Dawidowicz.* New York: Behrman House, 1978. A vivid retelling of Lucy Dawidowicz's monumental study of the Holocaust.

Joseph Bendersky, *A History of Nazi Germany.* Chicago: Nelson-Hall, 1985. A thorough look at the conditions that allowed the Nazis to gain control of the German government and win the allegiance of the German people.

Miriam Chaikin, *A Nightmare in History: The Holocaust 1933–1945.* New York: Clarion Books, 1987. A step-by-step account of Hitler's campaign to annihilate the Jews.

Olga Levy Drucker, *Kindertransport.* New York: Henry Holt, 1992. Born in Germany in 1927, the author of this book was just eleven years old when her parents sent her to England to avoid persecution by the Nazis. Drucker was one of ten thousand Jewish children saved in this operation.

William W. Lace, *The Nazis.* San Diego: Lucent Books, 1998. A profile of the political party that started out to redeem Germany after World War I but ended up disgracing and destroying it.

Milton Meltzer, *Rescue: The Story of How Gentiles Saved Jews in the Holocaust.* New York: HarperCollins, 1988. Although Gentile rescuers saved only thousands of Jews, compared with the millions who were slaughtered, Holocaust historian Milton Meltzer believes "they must not be forgotten. Their stories let us know that while there were victims, there were also heroes and heroines."

Anthony Read and David Fisher, *Kristallnacht: The Unleashing of the Holocaust.* New York: Peter Bedrick Books, 1989. Using eyewitness accounts, the authors describe the Night of Broken Glass that revealed the Nazi regime's intentions toward the Jews.

Earle Rice Jr., *The Final Solution.* San Diego: Lucent Books, 1998. Using numerous primary and secondary source quotations, Rice examines the causes and effects of the Nazi plan to murder the Jews of Europe.

Barbara Rogasky, *Smoke and Ashes: The Story of the Holocaust.* New York: Holiday House, 1988. Rogasky traces the Holocaust from the roots of anti-Semitism in medieval Germany, through the rise of the Nazi Party and the murder of 6 million Jews, to the end of World War II and the Nuremberg trials. The comprehensive book is richly illustrated with period photographs.

Works Consulted

Yehuda Bauer, *A History of the Holocaust.* New York: Franklin Watts, 1982. A complete history of the murder of 6 million European Jews, written by one of the most acclaimed Holocaust scholars of our time.

Ezra Ben Gershom, *David: Testimony of a Holocaust Survivor.* New York: Berg, 1988. The firsthand account of a young boy growing up in Nazi Germany. Ben Gershom describes the harassment he faced at school, his struggle to get an education once Jews were thrown out of the school system, how he and his family coped with the welter of anti-Jewish legislation, and how he escaped deportation and death.

Eugene Davidson, *The Trial of the Germans: Nuremberg 1945–1946.* New York: Macmillan, 1966. An in-depth look at the trial of the twenty-two major Nazi war criminals before the International Military Tribunal. This book provides a glimpse into the workings of the mind of Wilhelm Frick, who helped write the Nuremberg Laws.

Lucy S. Dawidowicz, *The War Against the Jews 1933–1945.* New York: Holt, Rinehart, and Winston, 1975. The premier work on the Nazi drive to make Europe *Judenrein,* free of Jews. Traces, in masterful detail, the roots of anti-Semitism, provides a complete discussion of anti-Jewish legislation in Germany and the occupied countries, and gives a complete history of the Holocaust.

Oswald Dutch, *Hitler's 12 Apostles.* New York: Robert M. McBride, 1940. Written in the period between the passage of the Nuremberg Laws and the full onslaught of the Holocaust, this work provides biographical data on the twelve leading Nazis of the time. It contains a fascinating portrait of Wilhelm Frick and also shows how the way we perceive the Nazi state has changed over time.

Raphael S. Ezekiel, *The Racist Mind: Portraits of American Neo-Nazis and Klansmen.* New York: Penguin Books, 1995. The product of a sociology professor's interviews with leaders and ordinary members of a number of neo-Nazi and Ku Klux Klan organizations. Ezekiel explains what leads people to become involved with hate groups, and outlines how they could be led into other, less-dangerous organizations.

Alex Grobman and Daniel Landes, eds., *Genocide: Critical Issues of the Holocaust.* Chappaqua, NY: Rossel Books, 1983. A companion to the film *Genocide,* this book offers a series of essays on various aspects of the Nazi period and the Holocaust.

Leonard Gross, *The Last Jews in Berlin.* New York: Simon and Schuster, 1982. Several thousand Jews survived the Holocaust in the Nazi capital by living in hiding or posing as non-Jews. Gross details the lives of several Jewish "U-boats" who managed to live in Berlin through the end of the war, as well as some who were not successful in their attempts to go underground.

Ingo Hasselbach and Tom Reiss, *Führer-Ex; Memoirs of a Former Neo-Nazi.* New York: Random House, 1996. The autobiography of one of the leaders of the East German neo-Nazi movement, written after he disavowed his former beliefs and left the organization. Hasselbach explains both what forces attracted him to neo-Nazism and what ultimately led him to leave it.

Paul Johnson, *A History of the Jews.* New York: Harper & Row, 1987. A concise history of four thousand years of Jewish history. Johnson provides an imminently readable discussion of the historical forces behind anti-Semitism, the rise of Adolf Hitler and his party, and the course of its assault on the Jews.

Helmut Krausnik et al., *Anatomy of the SS State.* New York: Walker, 1965. Shows how the Nazis reshaped the German bureaucracy, law enforcement system, and military to meet their own needs. Demonstrates how the reconstituted German government was used to suppress the Germans and oppress those it labeled enemies.

Daniel Lang, *A Backward Look: Germans Remember.* New York: McGraw-Hill, 1979. Interviews with Germans who lived through the Nazi era by an American visitor to the country.

Claude Lanzmann, *Shoah: An Oral History of the Holocaust.* New York: Pantheon Books, 1985. A companion piece to the film of the same name, *Shoah* creates a picture of a time that is almost impossible for those who did not live through it to imagine by using the words of those who did.

Werner Maser, *Hitler's Mein Kampf: An Analysis.* London: Faber and Faber, 1970. Maser, who has written several books about Hitler, attempts in this one to understand Hitler's thinking by examining the book he wrote in prison. Maser quotes liberally from *Mein Kampf,* and provides the historical background and psychological insight needed to understand the working of Hitler's mind.

Milton Meltzer, *Never to Forget: The Jews of the Holocaust.* New York: HarperCollins, 1976. A collection of first-person accounts of the Holocaust that shows how Europe's Jews reacted to the threat of extermination, with an emphasis on efforts at resistance.

John Mendelson, *The Holocaust: Selected Documents in Eighteen Volumes.* New York: Garland, 1982. A compendium of primary source material from the archives of the Third Reich.

Bezalel Narkiss, ed., *Picture History of the Jewish Civilization.* Jerusalem: Massada, 1978. Richly illustrated guide to Jewish history. Provides numerous examples of the Christian roots of anti-Semitic ideologies.

Joseph E. Persico, *Nuremberg: Infamy on Trial.* New York: Penguin Books, 1994. A description of the proceedings of the International Military Tribunal held in Nuremberg after World War II. Particularly valuable for its descriptions of Wilhelm Frick, one of the central authors of the Nuremberg Laws. Provides interesting insight into the behavior of the top Nazis once they lost power.

Harold E. Quinley and Charles Y. Glock, *Anti-Semitism in America.* New York: Macmillan, 1979. An examination of the persistence of anti-Semitism in the United States, this book offers statistical data that illuminate the pervasiveness of anti-Semitism and cast light on both its roots and its outcome in people's belief systems.

Hugh Rawson and Margaret Miner, eds., *The New International Dictionary of Quotations.* New York: NAL Penguin, 1986. An anthology of famous quotations.

Howard Morley Sachar, *The Course of Modern Jewish History.* New York: Dell, 1958. A comprehensive overview of European Jewish history from the eighteenth century to the years after the founding of Israel.

William L. Shirer, *The Rise and Fall of the Third Reich: A History of Nazi Germany.* New York: Simon and Schuster, 1960. Written by the CBS Radio correspondent in Berlin from the mid-1930s until December 1940, this extensive book (over a thousand pages) traces in vivid detail the Nazi period of German history. It is particularly valuable because it depends on Shirer's firsthand knowledge and experience, as well as the several years he spent researching the documents the Nazis left behind.

Index

pagan religions, 80
Palestine (Israel), 21, 23, 45, 50, 71–73, 81
Passover, 39–40
Paulus, Heinrich, 45
Persico, Joseph, 27–28
Pfundtner, Hans, 29–30, 35
pogroms, 40–41, 58
Poland, 49, 56, 61, 68, 79
  citizens killed in, 66
  Jews in, 53
political dissenters, 32
pornography, 51
Protestant Reformation, 71

Rabinowicz, Chaim, 36
"racial scientists," 57
racists, 73, 78
Räder, Erich, 60, 72
rape, 51
Ravensbrück concentration camp, 20
Reich Citizenship Law, 31–32, 55–57, 76, 84
Reichsbank, 22
Reichstag, 25, 27, 31–33, 51
Reinhardt, Max, 46
Reisser, Gabriel, 45
religion, 38–39, 70–71, 80–81
reparations, 72
Roman Catholic Church. *See* Catholic Church
Roman Empire, 38–39
Rosenberg, Alfred, 30, 47
Rosenthal, Gert, 58
Rosenthal, Max, 58
Russia, 49, 64, 83
  citizens killed in, 66

SA (*Sturmabteilung*), 13, 15–16, 27
Sachar, Howard Morley, 23, 63
Sachsenhausen concentration camp, 20
Sara (name of German Jews), 56
Schacht, Hjalmar, 22
Schicklgruber, Anna, 31
Schutzstaffel. *See* SS
Science of Racism, 30
SD (*Sicherheitsdienst*), 62
Second Crusade, 41
Second Degree. *See Mischlinge*
Second Vatican Council, 71
secret police (Gestapo), 34, 60, 70
separation of public facilities, 74–75
Serbia, 49, 77
Serbs, 77–78, 80
sexual relationships, 33
  see also extramarital intercourse
Sicherheitsdienst. See SD
Sippenforscher, 44
Sippenforschung (German Department for
  Family Research), 44
Sixth Ecumenical Council, 39
Sobibor concentration camp, 32, 48, 66, 69
social Darwinism (eugenics), 43
South Africa, 75–77

"special treatment," 68
SS (*Schutzstaffel*), 15–16, 44, 62, 65, 68
Stahmer, Otto, 62
Star of David, 8, 34, 56, 60, 62
sterilization, 28, 48, 58, 80
stolen art, 79
Streicher, Julius, 51
Stuckart, Wilhelm, 29, 31, 35
Sturmabteilung. See SA
suicide, 62, 80
swastika, 25, 34
Swiss banks, 79

T-4 project, 48
Theresienstadt concentration camp, 32–33,
  62
Third Reich, 28, 32, 54, 70–71, 78
Thomas, Ruth, 58, 61
Torah, 54
Treaty of Versailles, 49–52
Treblinka concentration camp, 32, 48, 63,
  66, 69
Truth and Reconciliation Commission, 77
Tuskegee Study of Untreated Syphilis in the
  Negro Male, 75

Übermensch (superman), 43
United States, 49, 74, 82

Vernichtung durch Arbeit (elimination
  through work), 62
Vernichtungslagern. See concentration
  camps
Volk (people), 47–49, 80
*Von die Juden und ihren Lügen (On the Jews
  and Their Lies)* (Luther), 71

Wannsee Conference, 29, 69
War Against the Jews, 1933–1945, The
  (Dawidowicz), 17, 20, 28, 44
Warsaw, 53, 56, 63–64
Wasserman, August von, 12
Wehrmacht, 60, 65
Weimar Republic, 50
Weizmann, Chaim, 45
Wenn Ich der Kaiser Wär (If I Were King)
  (Class), 20
"We Remember: A Reflection of the Shoah
  (Holocaust)," 71
Wessel, Horst, 11
William II, 49–50
"will to power," 43
World War I, 10, 12, 32, 49–50, 72
World War II, 12, 25, 32, 50, 56, 58, 66, 72,
  74, 80

Yugoslavia, 66, 77–78, 80

Zeppelin Field, 25
Zionism, 21, 23, 34, 45
Zyklon-B, 65

Picture Credits

About the Author

Amy Newman is an author, educator, and editor. Born in Augsburg, Germany, she now lives in Vista, California. This is her first book.